SOUL AUDIT

A NOT-SO-PERFECT, BROADLY SPIRITUAL (OR NOT) GUIDE TO LIVING IN ALIGNMENT

KIRK SHEPPARD

FOOT IN MOUTH
publishing

ISBN 979-8-9920318-6-7

For Ruthie.

Who took my chair—and changed what I saw.

"To thine own self be true."

WILLIAM SHAKESPEARE

CONTENTS

CHAPTER 1
NOTHING TO BE AFRAID OF

In my work as a therapist, I've sat with hundreds—maybe thousands—of people across offices, clinics, schools, and hospitals. Different ages. Different backgrounds. Different kinds of pain. But one thing shows up almost every time: the version of themselves they *want* to be rarely matches the version they're actually living.

Sometimes the gap is small—a matter of timing, or courage, or clarity. Other times, it's wide enough to feel like a double life. But whatever shape it takes, the cost is the same: disconnection, exhaustion, and that nagging sense that something just doesn't fit.

Whether their presenting problem is depression or anxiety, situational stress, PTSD, or a personality disorder, the common denominator is always the same: something in their life isn't lining up with the rest of who they are.

There are plenty of screening tools and assessments out there—and a million self-help books, too. Many of them are excellent and deeply helpful. But I've yet to find one that names and frames what I keep seeing: the quiet ache of living out of sync. The misalignment of the soul.

So I wrote my own.

It's imperative to know that when I talk about the soul, I'm not making a theological argument. I'm talking about the core of you—the part that knows when something is off, even if you can't explain it yet. Whether you call it your spirit, your wiring, your intuition, or just your gut, it counts. You don't need to believe anything mystical for this work to matter. You just have to believe that you're more than the roles you play.

I used to laugh when coworkers panicked about audits. As a new supervisor, I thought, "Perfect—someone's coming in to do the hard work of finding what's broken so I can actually fix it." I understood why the word made people tense, but I never saw audits as threats. **I saw them as flashlights.** They didn't create problems—they revealed them.

And once you can see clearly, you get to decide what stays, what goes, and what gets realigned.

That's what we're doing here.

No judgment. Just light.

You don't need to overhaul your life to move toward alignment. But you do have to start noticing where the performance ends—and where you begin.

WHAT WAS YOUR NAME?

When people find out that I used to be involved in professional wrestling, they ask me, "What was your wrestling name?" They're expecting some kind of character—a gimmick, a persona with a flashy name and a backstory.

And I get it. That's part of the job. Wrestling is about illusion. The goal is to convince the audience that what they're seeing is real—even when it's not. Most wrestlers invent characters to sell the story: flashy names, exaggerated personas, total separation between who they are in the ring and who they are at home.

But I didn't.

I used my real name. I didn't need a crazy gimmick or a mask or an alter ego. The guy you saw in the ring? That was me. Turned up louder, sure —more intense, more bombastic—but still me.

And here's the wild part: for a long time, the pro wrestling locker room was the only place in my life where I was fully out as gay.

In a world built on secrets, the part of me I was most ashamed of was known—and not a big deal.

I like to think the reason the crowd loved me and hated me and loved to hate me was because I wasn't pretending. I was magnifying. I took the parts of myself that fit the moment and put them on display. People responded to that. If there's one thing an audience knows how to do, it's spot a fake—and they're brutal when they do.

Not everyone took that approach.

There was a guy on the roster who was incredible in the ring—tough, magnetic, completely convincing. But he didn't just play a role; he lived in it. Most of the locker room didn't even know his real name, and that's how he wanted it. He kept his life behind the curtain completely separate.

He was exceptional at being the character. But outside the ring, things fell apart. Legal trouble. Broken relationships. Whatever was going on behind the curtain clearly wasn't working.

When you live that far out of alignment, it catches up with you. You might get applause, but you won't find peace.

That's what this book is about.

Soul alignment is the process of noticing where you're performing— and choosing instead to live with honesty. It's about shrinking the gap between who you are and how you show up in the world—at work, at home, in relationships, and even in your own head.

It matters because misalignment wears us down. It makes us anxious, disconnected, exhausted. But when we live in alignment, we feel more grounded, more present, more free. That's what we're aiming for—not perfection, just resonance.

The goal isn't to fix everything. It's to take an honest look at your life and figure out where things aren't lining up. Where you're performing instead of living. Where you've been pretending so long it feels normal. Where something in your gut keeps whispering, *"This isn't it."*

I'm not writing this as an academic expert on the topic. I'm speaking from experience. Because wrestling wasn't the only stage I stood on.

I've always existed in spaces where people perform—church pews, theatres, counseling offices. I used to think they were totally separate worlds: the ring, the stage, the therapy room. But over time, I realized they were all showing me the same thing. When people are out of alignment with who they really are—when they're doing instead of being—it hurts. And when they stop pretending and start to tell the truth? That's when healing starts.

I used to pretend to fight in UAW Halls, and I used to lead worship services in church sanctuaries—where I never felt safe to be fully me. Now, as a therapist, I help people get honest with themselves and the world around them. I also write plays and books, review theatre, and go to Disney World more often than most adults probably should.

I know it's an odd résumé. But it's mine. And it's what shaped this book. After all, twenty-one years of providing therapy to others has taught me a heck of a lot about myself.

Soul alignment isn't a theory for me—it's something I've lived, wrestled with, and watched others fight for, too. This book is full of those stories. They're weird. They're real. And I hope they help you find your own way to wholeness.

So how do you know if you're out of alignment?

By asking hard questions.

Together, we're going to walk through what I call a soul audit. We'll take inventory. Notice what fits and what doesn't. Look at how you're spending your energy and your time and with whom—and see whether any of it reflects who you really are. We'll get honest about what needs to stay and what needs to go.

It won't be easy, but it'll be worth it.

Because here's what I know: the most meaningful thing I've done—onstage, in therapy, or in my own life—was to stop performing and start aligning.

ONE VERSION, EVERYWHERE

If wrestling was the only place I didn't have to hide, then I had a lot of catching up to do everywhere else.

I didn't set a firm deadline, but I knew I had to come out before Cincinnati Pride. It had been on my mind for over a year, and all the "good" reasons not to were gone. The Christian university I taught at had closed, so there was no job to lose. I'd mostly let go of the guilt and shame, even if I hadn't fully figured out how to reconcile my faith with my sexuality. But staying quiet wasn't about integrity anymore. It was about fear.

If you've read *Jesus & Me*, you already know part of this story. That book was about faith deconstruction and learning to question the systems that shaped me.

This one is broader.

While *Jesus & Me* explored the beginnings of soul alignment, this book looks at a wider landscape—focusing on what happens when who you are and how you live finally start to match.

My life at the time was strategically compartmentalized. A few friends knew. A couple coworkers. Wrestling people knew. Some clients, when I felt it was relevant to their care. But with every person I told, I became the gatekeeper of that information. I had to track who knew and who didn't—like I was managing a classified document instead of just being a person.

And the more walls I built to keep things separate, the less safe I felt in any space.

I stayed especially guarded at Cincinnati Christian University, where coming out could've cost me my education—and later, my job.

But it wasn't just there.

I learned early that being different came with consequences. I was sent to therapy after my porn stash was discovered in a filing cabinet I thought I'd locked. (To be clear, "stash" meant one video I'd ordered from the internet. See? Even now I feel the need to clarify, just in case you're judging me.)

Spoiler alert: the therapy didn't take. Still gay.

I've felt the backlash even from something as simple as sharing a video of Alex Newell performing with the Boston Gay Men's Chorus with my teenage niece. The vibe was very much, *"How dare you expose her to something so gay."*

As if teenagers from small towns are somehow insulated from people like me—like we're some exotic species that only shows up in cities with drag brunch and a SoulCycle.

For most of my life, I learned to compartmentalize. To manage risk. To minimize rejection. To stay safe.

But at some point, hiding started to feel heavier than honesty.

I came out publicly at 45. I wrote a Facebook post. At first, I used the privacy settings to share it with a curated group—one more attempt to control the fallout. But halfway through, I thought, "This isn't alignment. This is still performance." So I made it public.

Then I logged off, jumped into bed, and pulled the covers over my head.

Minutes later, my friend David called to say he was proud of me. Comments poured in—supportive, affirming, and honestly overwhelming. If anyone disapproved, they had the sense to keep it to themselves. Apparently the closet door was unlocked the whole time. I just needed a little courage—and more rainbow emojis than I thought existed.

That was the first time I felt what alignment really is. No more gatekeeping, no more code-switching. I was just... me. One version. Everywhere.

You don't have to come out to experience that kind of freedom. But whatever your version of compartmentalization looks like, you probably know the toll it takes. A soul audit is simply a way to pause and ask: Where am I out of sync—and what would it feel like to stop performing?

Maybe you're the PTA mom who hates crafts but keeps gluing googly eyes to everything so no one catches on. Maybe you're in a job that sounds impressive at dinner parties but makes you cry in the parking lot twice a week. Maybe you've been pretending to love group texts, or church committees, or your friend's band. Alignment doesn't always mean coming out. Sometimes it just means admitting you don't like potlucks—and you never did.

JEANS IN BLUE ASH

When I first started in private practice, I worked out of an office in Harrison, a small town on the far western edge of Hamilton County. The culture there was laid back—lots of blue-collar workers, a surprising number of police officers and firefighters, and farmers from the surrounding rural areas. I felt comfortable in jeans. It matched the energy of the town, mirrored what my clients were wearing, and helped put people at ease.

Later, I started seeing clients in Blue Ash, a suburb north of Cincinnati. It had a different feel—more white collar, more upscale. So I adjusted. I swapped out my jeans for slacks and added collared shirts to the mix. I figured this is what people expected in that environment. I even made sure my belt matched my shoes. It was serious.

But something felt off. I was having a harder time keeping a full caseload —clients weren't sticking, and I couldn't figure out why. Until I realized the issue wasn't the location. It was me. I was presenting a version of myself I thought would be accepted instead of the one that actually worked.

So I went back to wearing jeans. And almost immediately, I noticed a difference. People stayed. They opened up more. They came back.

It turns out, my authenticity was more therapeutic than my wardrobe.

When I'm in alignment, I'm not performing—I'm showing up as the same person in every room I enter. I don't have to wonder if I'm "dressed right," or saying the right things, or matching some imaginary mold. There's an ease, a comfort, a groundedness to being fully myself. And oddly enough, it's when I'm most myself that I'm most effective— especially as a counselor.

That doesn't mean there aren't times I still catch myself slipping into roles or reaching for approval. But I've learned to pay attention to those moments—not with shame, but with curiosity. What am I trying to protect? Whose expectations am I meeting? And what would happen if I chose alignment instead?

Small misalignments often fly under the radar. But over time, they add up. They create tension we can't name, and fatigue we can't explain. And while it's tempting to think of "coming out" as a one-time event, the truth is, we're all coming out of something all the time—out of hiding, out of roles, out of costumes that no longer fit.

That's what soul alignment is about: not performing, not pleasing, not pretending—just being. In jeans, if that's what feels true.

HOW TO USE THIS BOOK

Each chapter explores a different aspect of soul alignment—things like values, emotion, boundaries, relationships, time, and purpose. The greatest hits. You'll find personal stories from my life and work, along with examples of how misalignment shows up in the real world—not in the abstract, but in jobs we hate, conversations we avoid, and roles we can't wait to outgrow.

And don't worry—all the client stories are fictionalized. They're based on real people and real dynamics, but no one is recognizable. That's intentional. They'll feel true—because they are—but without compromising anyone's privacy.

You'll see the word authenticity show up throughout this book—but it's not exactly the same thing as alignment. Authenticity is about being honest with yourself. Alignment is about *living that honesty out loud.*

I've met plenty of people who know exactly who they are—but still feel stuck, exhausted, or invisible. That's because authenticity without alignment still feels like performance. It's knowing the truth but not walking in it yet.

This book will hopefully help you close that gap.

At the end of each chapter, you'll find a Soul Audit Reflection—a short list of questions to help you notice what's working, what's not, and what might need some attention. It's like checking your emotional alignment—without needing a lift or a wrench.

Then you'll see a section called From the Audit to Action—a simple invitation to move from awareness into practice. Nothing dramatic. No vision boards required. Just small, doable changes. Alignment doesn't happen overnight, and frankly, it shouldn't. It's slow work—but it's good work.

While my version of misalignment involved staying in the closet too long, yours might involve people-pleasing, saying yes when you mean hell no, or chasing approval instead of purpose. Maybe you're tired of editing yourself. Maybe you're exhausted and not sure why. Whatever it looks like, the process is the same: notice, name it, adjust.

By the end of this book, I hope you feel more like yourself—and less like you're playing a role in someone else's story. Not perfectly aligned, but heading in the right direction, one honest step at a time.

SOUL AUDIT: ALIGNMENT

Alignment doesn't always require massive change. But it does ask for honesty—especially in the small, daily ways we shape-shift without even realizing it.

Check all that apply:

- ☐ I adjust my personality depending on who I'm around
- **☐ I can name at least one space where I feel fully myself**
- ☐ I've played a version of myself that felt more "acceptable" than real
- **☐ I've experienced moments where I felt fully at ease—no editing, no effort**
- ☐ I second-guess myself before I speak, even with people I know
- **☐ I know the difference between feeling seen and being observed**

FROM THE AUDIT TO ACTION

Awareness

Now look at what you checked. The ones in **bold** are great signs; the non-bolded ones are opportunities to make changes

You don't need to make a grand announcement or throw away your khakis. Just start noticing the micro-moments where you edit, shrink, or shape-shift.

Ask yourself:

- *Where am I most tempted to perform?*
- *Who brings out the realest version of me?*
- *Where do I feel drained after showing up—like I left part of myself behind?*

PRACTICE

This week, pick one small area to un-perform:

- *Say what you really want to eat, even if it's different from the group.*
- *Wear the jeans.*
- *Let your laugh be unfiltered.*

Alignment isn't about overhauling your life. It's about letting your insides match your outsides—one moment at a time.

CHAPTER 2
LEARNED, LIVED, OR LEFT BEHIND?

THE FIRST DOMAIN in the soul auditing process is *values*.

Most people can identify a few things they value. But I'm not talking about sentimental items; I mean the principles and qualities that feel important. Our values drive decisions, shape relationships, fill the calendar, and determine where our money and energy go.

If I say, "What do you value?" you might list things that are meaningful or useful to you: family, success, health, maybe stability. But when I ask, "What are your values?"—I'm asking what you live by.

For further clarification, the question, "What do you value?" changes with context. For example, I value rest more after a week of hustle. I value alone time the minute I leave a crowded party.

These answers reveal immediate needs, but they don't define who I am.

But my values don't change so easily. The importance I place on independence isn't variable based on circumstance; it's always true that I cherish doing what I want when I want—whether I'm home, at work, or on vacation.

Most of us didn't consciously choose our earliest values. We absorbed them from family, culture, or community. Some we carry proudly. Others we outgrow—or never really agreed with to begin with.

I grew up on a farm with mud-caked boots. I had chores like shoveling manure and bailing hay. I always had a strong sense that manual labor was both expected and respected. My stepdad could fix anything with duct tape and determination. Strength, sweat, and showing up—those were the currency of character.

But I was wired differently.

It wasn't that I was lazy (though I'm sure someone called me that once or twice); I just gravitated toward tasks that made me think. I'd rather figure out how to do something more efficiently than power through it. If there was a smarter way, I wanted to find it.

My grandfather said it a lot: "Work smarter, not harder." I clung to that like a permission slip. Not because I didn't want to pull my weight—but because I knew my strengths lay somewhere outside of using my back.

That's the thing about values: some are passed down. Others rise up from inside. And the tension between who we were raised to be and who we actually are often reveals misalignment.

For me, that tension showed up early. I didn't always have words for it, but I felt it. I felt it when I'd rather read than mow. When I wrote stories in the corner of the family Christmas party instead of playing board games with everyone else. Or when I performed full-on concerts in the solitude of my bedroom while my sister socialized with her friends.

Instead of playing football, I edited the school newspaper. When it came time for prom, I took the yearbook camera instead of a date. Instead of pouring my energy into Calculus and Physics, I preferred to read and write stories that weren't assigned by any teacher.

Maybe your version looked different. But think back—were there moments you felt misaligned, even before you had the language for it? That quiet instinct that said, "This isn't me"—that matters.

No one had to tell me I was weird. I knew it. And I could feel the disapproval without hearing the words. In my mind, being misunderstood was the same as being judged.

As a teenager, I internalized that judgment. I believed my version of contributing to the world wasn't valuable. That creativity, emotional sensitivity, and insight weren't as legit as grit and grime and sweat on my brow.

But I've since learned that they are.

That's why soul alignment takes more than honesty. It takes courage. The willingness to admit that you might not value what your culture, your family, or your faith community told you to.

It also takes curiosity. Because some of your values might surprise you. They might feel like they came from nowhere. Or maybe they've always been there, waiting for a name.

This is where nature and nurture wrestle. And the truth is, they both win. Our values are shaped by the people around us—but sometimes, they also emerge from something deeper we've always known.

Are values shaped by how we're raised? Absolutely. But some are like fingerprints. We're born with them. We don't choose them. We uncover them.

THE ONES YOU GOT, THE ONES YOU WANT, AND THE ONES THAT HAUNT YOU

Before we move on, let's name what we're talking about.

Not all values are the same. Some are handed down like a family recipe. Others are aspirational—they look good on paper. Some are running your life without your consent. And some you've tried to walk away from but they still whisper in the hallway.

Here's a quick breakdown:

1. Inherited Values Taught directly or absorbed through family, religion, or culture. They're often presented as "just the way things are."

Example: You believe hard work is everything because your parents said so. Taking a nap makes you feel guilty.

2. Unconscious Values These are absorbed under pressure, fear, or survival. They become your operating system.

Example: You always say yes, even when you're exhausted. Somewhere you learned that being helpful = being safe. You're valuing approval without knowing it.

3. Aspirational Values The values you want to have. You admire them. You list them on your vision board. But if they're not showing up in your calendar or habits, they might be more about who you hope to be.

Example: You say you value mindfulness but have doom-scrolled TikTok every night this week instead of meditating.

4. Actual Values

These are the ones you're living—the values that consistently show up in your actions and instincts.

Example: You value creativity, and it shows. You write, paint, curate playlists, or organize your bookshelf by theme and color.

5. Haunting Values

These are the values you've outgrown or actively rejected, but they still echo. They show up as hesitation, guilt, or second-guessing. You've left the building, but the wiring remains.

Example: You've walked away from church, but still feel anxious skipping the Easter service. You affirm body positivity—but still flinch when your jeans don't fit. You believe love is love, but hear old voices when your child comes out as pansexual.

Key distinctions:

- Inherited values are taught.
- Unconscious values are absorbed.
- Aspirational values are imagined.
- Actual values are practiced.

- Haunting values are rejected—but still echo.

Values aren't usually inherently good or bad. But if you don't know where your values came from—or whether they still serve you—you'll follow them by default. And that can be terrible.

So ask: Where did they come from? Are they helping or harming? Who gave them a key to your house in the first place?

FIRST HONEST GLIMPSE

This is your first real check-in.

Before we go further, sit with this:

- *What's one value you were raised to believe in—but that no longer feels true for you?*
- *What's one value you've always held, even if no one taught it to you?*

No scorecard. No perfect answer. Just a chance to reflect.

YOU SAY YOU VALUE HEALTH (BUT ALSO CHEESE FRIES)

So how do you figure out what your actual values are?

Most people start with what they think they *should* value: honesty, family, faith, kindness, health, service, savings. Like writing what the teacher—or therapist—wants you to value.

But the soul doesn't respond to "shoulds." It responds to truth.

That's why I tell people to look at their daily lives instead. Where does your time go? What do you protect? What energizes or drains you?

Those things tell the truth.

For example: I say I value saving money. But my bank account says otherwise. I might aspire to value it. But I'm not living it.

Or this: I say I value serving others. But if you ask me to help you move, I suddenly vanish. Maybe I value helpfulness—but only in certain ways. It's definitely not while wedging a sectional through a stairwell.

Clarity doesn't come from declarations. It comes from observation.

So, *what's one value you claim, but haven't lived lately?* Can you name a recent moment when your choices didn't match that value? **No shame. Just information.** That's where alignment starts: **noticing the gaps.**

I had a client who told me he spent two and a half days crafting a values list. When he brought it in, I looked it over and said, "You didn't put 'getting it right' on your list. Did you realize that was a value you hold?"

His list was beautiful. But it reflected who he wanted to be, not who he actually was. There's nothing wrong with aspiration. But alignment starts with honesty. Aspirational values are about who you want to be. Actual values are about who you are right now.

It's important to name both. Just don't confuse them.

Why? Because when you mistake an aspirational value for an actual one, you set a standard you're not aligned with. And that's where **shame** creeps in.

I say I value health—but I stay up late, skip meals, and avoid exercise. I don't just feel tired—I feel like a failure. Instead of adjusting the standard, I punish myself for not living up to it.

Or I say I value relationships, but my schedule leaves no room for connection. Every missed text or canceled plan makes me feel guilty—even though what I actually value right now might be independence, or rest, or healing.

There's nothing wrong with that.

But when your actions don't match your identity, you lose trust in yourself.

Misalignment doesn't start with a dramatic shift. It starts with small, repeated choices that chip away at who you are.

This chapter matters because identifying your actual values—even if they surprise or disappoint you—is the only way to live a life that feels congruent—and honest.

THIS IS YOUR LIFE (AND IT'S TELLING ON YOU)

So let's figure out what your actual values are.

Not the ones you think you should have. Not the ones that look good on a bumper sticker or a dating profile. The ones showing up in your day to day right now.

Let's start with some examples. These are a few values people often hold —not because they sound noble, but because they show up in real deci- sions, gut instincts, and everyday priorities:

- Stability
- Adventure
- Creativity
- Rest
- Connection
- Independence
- Justice
- Security
- Growth
- Curiosity
- Generosity

- Authenticity
- Play
- Achievement
- Wisdom
- Compassion
- Order
- Flexibility
- Freedom
- Excellence
- Kindness
- Privacy
- Belonging

If a few of those immediately stand out, make a mental note.

And if a few make you roll your eyes, make a note of those, too. Sometimes resistance reveals just as much as resonance.

Now let's do a quick values audit. No pressure. No scorecard. Just a bit of observation.

The "How You Spend a Week" Exercise

Let's zoom in on your actual life—not what you meant to do, not what you told yourself you value, but what actually happened.

Think about your last seven days:

- Where did your time go?
- Where did your energy go?
- What did you prioritize, protect, or avoid?

You don't need a spreadsheet. Just observe. Patterns will emerge.

Now go deeper. Ask yourself:

- Where did I choose to spend the most time?
- What did I make space for—even when I was tired?
- What did I consistently avoid—even if I said it mattered?

Those are your values in motion. Not the ones you list on a vision board —the ones that are already making choices for you.

Maybe you say you value integrity, but you told three little fibs this week to keep the peace. Maybe what you're really valuing right now is harmony.

Maybe you say you value curiosity, but every free moment went to rewatching a comfort show. Maybe novelty isn't your priority right now —and maybe that's okay.

Sometimes your needs and values compete.

Sometimes your needs *reveal* your values.

YOU CAN'T WORK THE GIMMICK IF YOU DON'T DO THE WORK

As part of my role in pro wrestling, I used to help train aspiring pro wrestlers. And one of them—let's call him Timothy—had big dreams.

He wanted to be in WWE. He said it all the time. He posted in character on Facebook like he was already there, cutting promos, sharing "insider" catchphrases, living the gimmick. But here's the thing: Tim skipped workouts—but definitely not meals. He barely showed up to training. He only showed up once a week, and phoned it in when he was there. He didn't train. He didn't ask questions. He didn't even show up consistently to do security at the live shows—which was kind of a requirement.

He *said* he valued being a wrestler. But what he really valued was the *idea* of being one. He didn't want the grind. He wanted the entrance music, the merch table, and the admiration.

His values weren't just aspirational. They were borderline delusional.

And he's not uncommon.

Contrast that with my friend Chad. When he was starting out, he went to the gym *every day*. He studied tape—of himself, his peers, and of the wrestling greats. He learned how to work a crowd *and* take care of his body. He paid attention. Took notes. Showed up early. Stayed late. Eventually, he got signed to a contract in New Japan Pro Wrestling as "Karl Anderson," and later wrestled in WWE.

Yeah, he got lucky at a few key moments. But that luck wouldn't have meant anything if his values hadn't already aligned with his work ethic.

One guy wanted to be a wrestler.

The other guy *became* one.

NOT A CONTRACT—JUST A MIRROR

So, let's distill it.

Look back over what came up for you in this chapter. Maybe a few values stood out from the earlier list. Maybe something surfaced when you thought about how you've been spending your time, money, or energy this week. Maybe you're still not totally sure—and that's okay.

This isn't about getting it perfect. It's about getting closer.

Try This:

Choose three to five values that feel true *right now*. Not aspirational. Not idealized. Just honest.

If you're stuck, try finishing this sentence a few different ways:

"The days I feel most like myself are the days I…"

- *get to create something from scratch*
- *connect deeply with one person instead of a room full of people*
- *don't feel rushed*
- *make someone laugh*

- *finish what I said I'd do*
- *learn something new*

Now ask yourself:

What value is at the heart of that moment?

Those are your guideposts.

They help you make decisions, set boundaries, and come back to yourself when life gets loud.

But here's the spoiler: your values will shift—or at least evolve.

This isn't a one-time activity. It's a lifelong practice.

As you grow, heal, lose, change careers, end relationships, or build new ones—your values may sharpen, rearrange, or surprise you. That's not a problem. That's the process.

That's why we're doing this work now. Not to create a fixed list, but to build the habit of paying attention.

Alignment isn't something you achieve once.

It's something you return to—over and over again.

Want to go one step further?

Write down your current top 3–5 values somewhere you'll see them:

A sticky note. A journal. Your phone's lock screen.

Don't treat it like a contract.

Treat it like a mirror.

SOUL AUDIT: VALUES

We inherit a lot—beliefs, traditions, even definitions of what "good" looks like. But alignment asks us to stop and ask: *Is this value actually mine?*

Check all that apply:

☐ I've been living by values I never consciously chose

☐ I know what's most important to me—but I don't always honor it

☐ There's a gap between what I say I care about and how I spend my time

☐ **I've started rethinking some of the values I was raised with**

☐ **I can name a few values that feel deeply true—even if they're unconventional**

☐ **I'm willing to let go of inherited beliefs that no longer serve me**

Now pause and look at what you checked. What's being revealed? You don't have to reject your past. You just have to choose what gets to stay.

FROM AUDIT TO ACTION

Awareness

Misalignment often begins in silence—not because you're lying, but because you're still living someone else's values.

Start small:

- *What's one value you grew up believing was non-negotiable?*
- *Where did it come from? Family? Church? School?*
- *Do you still believe it—or has it started to shift?*

Now, take a second look:

Name one value you live by today—the kind that shows up naturally in how you think, love, spend, or serve—even if you've never called it a value before.

Finally:

Notice if there's any value you've consciously rejected, but still feel a pull toward out of guilt or habit. (That's haunting, not choosing.)

You don't have to fix anything today. Just observe. Let yourself be curious.

PRACTICE

Pick one real value that's already showing up in your life—the kind that didn't need a resolution or a gold star to exist.

Now, choose one tiny action this week to honor it intentionally. For example:

- *If rest matters, protect your bedtime.*
- *If connection matters, reach out to a friend just because.*
- *If curiosity matters, make space to read, learn, or wander.*

Alignment isn't about having the "right" values.

It's about letting your actual values matter—and letting yourself live like you believe them.

CHAPTER 3
FEELINGS ARE NOT THE PROBLEM

IT WAS SUPPOSED to be a quick stop at Arby's.

I was on my way to Kings Island and needed something to eat. But the person in front of me at the drive-thru was taking forever. It was a minivan—the kind that screams "Soccer practice and juice boxes"—and they seemed to be asking one thousand questions about curly fries. I watched as they handed something to the employee. Then they handed it back. Then they changed their order. The drive-thru worker leaned out to coo over a tiny dog in the passenger seat. I swear they were about to exchange phone numbers.

I could feel my blood pressure rising. "Oh come ON," I muttered.

Okay, not muttered. Said aloud. With the window down.

I was furious. I was hungry. I was in a rush. I was making judgments left and right. "Know what you want before you get in line!" I shouted toward the car in front of me. I was stewing in my own impatience— absolutely marinating in it.

And then I pulled up to the window.

The employee smiled and handed me my food.

"No charge," he said. "The guy ahead of you paid for it."

Silence.

Of course he did. All that back and forth . . some of it included treating me to roast beef and potato cakes.

I felt like the biggest jerk in the world—and also, somehow, like I'd been handed a cosmic reality check. Without a word, this stranger reminded me that my assumptions are often wrong, my emotions aren't always reliable, and my snap judgments are rarely kind.

I laughed. And then I said—because sometimes I talk to the Universe like that—"Okay. Point taken."

MESSAGES, NOT MALFUNCTIONS

That moment in the drive-thru taught me something important about emotions: they're fast, strong, and not always accurate.

In a matter of minutes, I went from mildly annoyed to full-blown furious—because I assumed I knew what was happening. I didn't. I had some information, but not the full story. And that's where a lot of us get misaligned: we treat emotions like facts instead of what they usually are —signals.

Emotions aren't always true. But they're still useful.

They're not something to fix. They're something to pay attention to.

When you feel something—anxiety, anger, sadness—it's usually trying to tell you something. That *something* doesn't have to be dramatic or life-changing. But it's worth noticing.

Anxiety might be alerting you to something that feels off or that there's danger pending.

Anger might be showing you a boundary that was crossed.

Sadness might be pointing to a loss or something that's been ignored.

But instead of listening, most of us were taught to shut those feelings down.

"Stay calm." "Don't cry." "Cheer up." "Be strong."

We learned to override emotion—to hide it, dismiss it, or flip a switch and act like we're fine.

That kind of response creates misalignment. Your body knows something's happening, but your brain is too busy performing the version of yourself that feels acceptable.

And that's exhausting.

In the drive-thru, I wasn't just mad—I was wrong. I didn't have the full story, and once I got it, the anger vanished. Replaced with embarrassment. And maybe a little gratitude for the reminder.

That's how feelings work. They move. They change. They shift as new information comes in.

You don't have to act on every emotion. But you do have to listen.

FROM RAMBO TO OPRAH

Let's talk about anger for a minute.

I think anger is one of the most misunderstood—and overused—emotions we've got. Not because it's not valid, but because it's rarely what we're actually feeling underneath.

Anger is *expressive* and *protective*. It sends a clear message:

"I'm not okay, and you need to back off."

It's the bodyguard emotion. It shows up to guard the stuff underneath —things like fear, sadness, disappointment, shame, or embarrassment.

Therapists call it a secondary emotion—it shows up after something more vulnerable that we're not sure how to express.

And for a lot of people—especially men—anger was the only emotion that was ever allowed. We were taught that strength means being in control. Unfazed. And if pushed, a little dangerous.

So what happens when we're sad? We get mad.

Scared? Mad.

Embarrassed? Overwhelmed? Powerless?

We get mad.

Because for many of us, anger was the only thing that ever fit the role we were taught to play. And let's be honest—it works. Anger gets people to back off. It makes us feel strong. It gives us something to do.

But strength isn't just intensity or action. It's also honesty. It's being able to say, "Actually, I'm hurt."

Or, "That really scared me."

Or, "I need a minute."

One of my jobs as a therapist is to help people go from **Rambo** to just a little bit closer to **Oprah**.

Not because I think you should start handing out free cars or Gucci bags or Jimmy Choo shoes.

But because Oprah embodies **emotional fluency**. She can be angry, soft, honest, firm, joyful, and clear—all at once.

EMPATH OR EXHAUSTED

I was talking with someone recently about a play we both saw, and they said, "I don't like sad shows. I don't want to feel bad." They weren't being dismissive. They consider themselves an empath—someone who feels things deeply, maybe more than most. I get that instinct. Who wants to sit in a dark room and watch someone suffer onstage, especially when we've already got enough heaviness of our own?

But I've been thinking about that conversation ever since.

Theatre is where I go to feel things. It's where I've learned how to hold sadness without falling apart. It's where I've realized that grief, longing, and loss aren't problems to be solved—they're invitations. They make us more human, not less.

Empathy is real. But lately, I've noticed how often the word 'empath' gets used like a diagnosis or a fixed personality type—like there are Feelers and Non-Feelers, and you're either one or the other.

But I don't think empathy works like that. I think it's a skill—one that develops over time, shaped by personality, experience, and environment. For a lot of people, being emotionally attuned wasn't a gift they were born with. It was a protective tactic. They learned to read the room before speaking. They got good at sensing when someone's mood shifted, because that kind of awareness helped them avoid conflict or stay safe. They became experts at managing other people's emotions because that's what the situation demanded.

That's not just intuition. That's survival.

And for the record—I believe in intuition. I believe in gut feelings, spiritual knowing, and the kinds of truths we can't always explain. But I also know that trauma can disguise itself as instinct. And sometimes the thing we call a gift is actually a defense.

So when someone says, "I'm an empath. I just can't handle sad stories," I don't hear emotional sensitivity. I hear nervous system fatigue. I hear someone who's been on high alert for too long and doesn't have space to carry more.

But what if sitting in a theatre and feeling something that isn't personal isn't dangerous? What if it's healing? Sadness in a safe space—where no one expects anything from you—might actually help you reconnect with something inside yourself. Because if you can feel sadness without trying to fix it, you might also be able to feel other things. You might create more space. For joy. For connection. For being fully human.

And here's something else worth remembering: you can't numb selectively. If you avoid sadness, you also dull joy. If you shut down pain, you lose access to wonder. If you avoid grief, you lose some of your capacity to love.

That's why emotional alignment isn't just about showing feelings—it's about allowing them, especially the ones that don't serve a clear purpose or the ones you were taught to push away.

As a therapist, I've sat with people who were grieving, angry, frozen, overwhelmed. And I've learned that it's not the emotion itself that breaks us down—it's the effort we spend trying to control it. It's the judgment. It's the internal story that says, "I shouldn't be feeling this," or "This is too much," or "I must be weak."

You're allowed to feel deeply. You're allowed to cry during a play, or a commercial, or in the cereal aisle at Kroger. That doesn't make you weak. I think it makes you brave.

And the more willing you are to feel what's real, the more clearly you'll recognize misalignment when it shows up. You stop performing emotions that feel acceptable and start honoring the ones that are actually true.

That doesn't make you a wimp. That makes you human.

SHE PICKED MY CHAIR ON PURPOSE

Ruthie showed up with a bandage on her hand and a chip on her shoulder.

She was referred to me after an industrial accident that left her hand severely damaged. Two of her fingers were crushed beyond repair, and a third was barely hanging on. She arrived to therapy with her hand still wrapped, the bandages holding her bones together. I was supposed to help her process the trauma.

Ruthie didn't want my help.

She was sharp-tongued and hostile. She called me a dumbass—often. If I asked how she was feeling, she'd roll her eyes. If I asked her to name an emotion, she'd say, "Hungry." Or "Irritated." Or, "I feel like going home."

At first glance, Ruthie looked emotionally shut down. But that wasn't it at all. She was on high alert every second. Watching me. Testing me. Measuring how safe I was.

And once she started talking, I understood why.

She told me stories about her mother—who once fired a shotgun at a man on a tractor just for fun. Who threatened to blow the sheriff's head off if he came around again. That was the kind of emotional climate Ruthie grew up in: explosive, volatile, unpredictable.

So Ruthie adapted. She armored up. She learned that emotions got you hurt—or hunted. That silence was safer than sorrow. That sarcasm could be a shield. That anger could pass for strength.

Ruthie was one of the most empathic people I've ever met. Not in the crystal-carrying, "I'm an empath" kind of way. But in the *I've-had-to-survive* kind of way.

She could read energy like radar. She could feel emotional threat before it entered the room. She also knew how to protect herself without lifting a finger. She was the first client who ever sat in my chair—forcing me to sit opposite from where I was used to. She knew that would disarm me—and give her the power she needed to feel safe.

And while she didn't seem "New Agey" in the slightest, she once told me she saw a figure of a man standing behind me—protective, quiet. She thought maybe it was my dad.

My dad died when I was six. She didn't know that.

At the time, I didn't know what to make of it. Was it intuition? Psychosis? Trauma perception? I've thought about it a lot since.

And here's where I've landed: if anyone could see what others can't, it's someone like Ruthie. Because when your whole life is built around detecting danger, you become fluent in things other people miss.

Ruthie became one of my favorite clients. And while she'd never admit it, I think she started to enjoy therapy a little bit. She was the kind of woman who—if anyone ever threatened to hurt me—would've gone full vigilante on them. One handed or not, I wouldn't fight her.

I think she liked me.

But she'd never say that out loud.

EMOTIONALLY ARMORED, NOT UNAVAILABLE

Ruthie reminded me that most people aren't emotionally unavailable—they're **emotionally armored**. They're not cold. They're scanning for safety, trying to stay in control, trying not to fall apart. What we read as sarcasm, anger, or shutdown is often something else entirely. It's grief with a defense mechanism. It's fear in disguise. It's tenderness that never got a chance to grow up.

Emotional alignment doesn't mean fixing your feelings—it means getting curious about them. We all have emotional habits: go-to reactions, default responses we've picked up over time, often without even realizing it.

You've learned by now that feelings aren't the problem. Pretending not to have them? That's misalignment.

Some people cry when they're angry. Some smile when they're hurt. Others go silent when they're scared, or get loud when they feel ashamed. These aren't character flaws. They're patterns. And the more you notice them, the more choice you have.

SOUL AUDIT: EMOTIONAL ALIGNMENT

Emotions aren't flaws. They're messages. Alignment means letting yourself feel—even when it's messy.

Check all that apply:

- ☐ I sometimes explain or justify my feelings instead of letting myself feel them.
- ☐ I've been told I'm "too emotional" or "not emotional enough"
- ☐ I feel uncertain or self-conscious when naming what I feel
- ☐ I have emotional habits I've noticed—like shutting down, overexplaining, or getting louder when I feel vulnerable
- ☐ I've started to notice patterns in when I feel most reactive or most disconnected
- **☐ I can name one emotion I've made peace with—even if it used to scare me**

Now pause and look at what you checked. What are your patterns trying to tell you? What's asking for understanding—not judgment?

This isn't a performance. It's a practice.

FROM THE AUDIT TO ACTION

Awareness

Your emotions are not flaws. They're info. Some of it's clear. Some of it's noisy. But all of it is worth paying attention to.

Ask yourself:

- *What emotion do I perform because it feels "allowed"?*
- *What feeling gets replaced by anger, silence, or sarcasm?*
- *What's an emotion I've misjudged as weakness—but maybe it's just under-practiced?*

Instead of asking, "Is this emotion valid?" ask, "What is this emotion trying to show me?"

Practice

Pick one emotion this week to get curious about. Just one. Not to fix—just to notice.

When it shows up, name it.

Instead of reacting, pause. Say (out loud if you want):

"This is just _____. It's not permanent. And it might be useful."

Optional bonus: write it down when it happens. That's your data set.

Alignment doesn't mean being calm or centered all the time. It means being honest.

And honesty starts by telling the truth about what you feel—even if no one ever taught you how.

CHAPTER 4
DON'T BE A JERK, AND ALSO DON'T BE A DOORMAT

BEFORE I EVER MET MY upstairs neighbor, I hated him.

Okay—hate might be a strong word. But when he moved in, it sounded like he was running a bowling alley. Or having sumo matches in his living room. Or just stomping around for the fun of it.

It was loud. And it was loud late.

I didn't want to be the guy who complains about every little thing, nor did I want to be the cranky neighbor from *Friends*. So instead of knocking on his door, I emailed the apartment manager and asked her to talk to him about how sound carries in the building. She said she would.

A few days later, I came home to a Ziploc bag of homemade cookies and a handwritten note that said, "Sorry for the recent noise." It was signed with his apartment number.

I was relieved. I emailed the manager to say thanks for handling it so gently.

She responded, "Oh—I never got a chance to talk to him."

Turns out, he'd figured it out on his own. And responded with kindness. Not defensiveness. Not denial. Just cookies.

Not to be outdone, I picked up a gift card to a local pizza place. I slipped it into a handmade Mickey Mouse card, wrote a "welcome to the building" note, and left my number in case he ever needed anything.

The next day, I got more cookies. And a new note that said to text anytime I wanted fresh bread or a refill on sweets.

That interaction taught me something: connection is often born in the space between *hesitation and grace.* It's easy to feel detached from people when we're annoyed by them. Or scared of them. Or unsure how they'll respond. And yet, every act of alignment—every time we choose curiosity over criticism, gentleness over performance—moves us closer to something real.

Relational alignment isn't only about romantic partners or family dynamics. It's also about neighbors. Baristas. Coworkers. Clients. People we barely know, but who cross our emotional radar all the time.

When we show up without armor, connection gets easier—and may result in cookies.

THE EXHALE AFTER THE DINNER PARTY

Relational alignment is when your relationships reflect who you really are—not who you think you need to be in order to be accepted. It's when your connections are rooted in truth, not performance. It's when you don't have to rehearse every conversation or wonder if you were "too much" or "not enough." When love doesn't feel like a transaction.

Many of us don't grow up knowing what that feels like. Instead, we learn how to *manage* people. We learn how to make ourselves likable. We figure out which parts of ourselves are "safe" to show and which ones are better off hidden. We learn to shrink or stretch depending on who we're with.

That's relational misalignment. It doesn't always look like conflict or dysfunction. Sometimes it just feels like *fatigue*.

You leave a dinner party and exhale like you've been holding your breath all night. You finish a phone call and realize you didn't say a single thing you actually meant. You say yes when your whole body is screaming no. You listen to someone vent for an hour and think, "Why do I feel like the trash can?"

Sometimes misalignment is obvious—like staying in a relationship that drains you. But sometimes it's subtle. Sometimes it sounds like:

"I'm not mad." "It's fine." "Whatever works for you." "I just want everyone to be happy."

Behind those words is a soul that's quietly disappearing.

When we abandon ourselves to stay connected to someone else, we're not really in relationship. We're in performance. And it's exhausting.

EASIER TO LOVE THAN TO KNOW

We all want to be loved. But being known? That's a different level of vulnerability.

To be loved is to be admired. But to be known means being seen in your inconsistencies, your contradictions, your everyday ordinariness—and still being chosen.

When someone really knows you, they see the stuff you usually hide. The mess. The tension. The unprocessed grief. The tired version of you who doesn't have anything clever to say.

That's the version most of us are scared to show. Because what if we show up like that and get rejected?

So we keep editing ourselves. We lead with our impressive parts. We perform the version of ourselves we think others can handle.

But the truth is, intimacy is impossible without honesty. And you can't feel aligned in a relationship if you're only offering a curated version of yourself.

Relational alignment requires risk. It means letting people in. It means choosing the discomfort of truth over the comfort of performance.

But that's where the good stuff lives.

Being loved is beautiful. Being known? That's freedom.

THE DISAPPEARING ACT

I met Debby during a season when her life was slowly unraveling — but she couldn't admit it yet.

Her husband was an alcoholic. Not abusive, but absent. He worked long hours, came home exhausted, and checked out — one beer, one television show, one missed conversation at a time.

Her teenage kids were growing up, pulling away in that natural but painful way teenagers do. They still loved her, but they didn't need her like they once had. And without their constant dependence, Debby felt like she was floating without an anchor.

So she poured herself into what she knew: service. Church volunteer committees. Meals for neighbors. Hours spent sitting with an elderly woman down the street whose own children rarely visited. She told herself she was being a good neighbor, a good Christian, a good woman. But underneath all that effort, something quieter was happening: Debby was disappearing.

In our early sessions, she rarely talked about herself. Instead, she asked about me. Complimented my shoes. Noticed when I looked tired. It was subtle, but it was a pattern — one I recognized instantly.

Caretaking was her currency. Offering support was how she tried to earn her space in the world. Even here, in a space meant for her healing, she instinctively tried to take care of me.

I let her, at first. Not because I didn't notice — but because meeting people where they are is sometimes the first real step toward change. Over time, I started gently naming the pattern. Not to shame her. But to offer a new truth:

"You don't have to earn your space here," I told her once. "You already have it."

Debby blinked back tears. She smiled. She changed the subject.

But something had started to shift.

QUICK CHECK-IN:

Think about your closest relationships—family, friends, work, romantic partners, community. Don't just consider who you are in those spaces. Ask yourself: Who do you become?

Do any of these roles feel familiar?

- **The Fixer:** You take on responsibility for everyone else's problems. You jump in before anyone asks. You feel anxious when things are unresolved—even if they're not yours to resolve.
- **The Peacemaker:** You avoid conflict. You'd rather keep things smooth than say how you really feel. You often say "it's fine" when it's not.
- **The Performer:** You're upbeat, polished, entertaining—even when you're hurting. You worry that if you stop smiling, people will stop staying.
- **The Caretaker:** You're always available. Always supportive.

Always showing up for others—sometimes at the expense of your own well-being.

- **The Rock:** You don't ask for help. You don't cry in front of people. You feel like you have to be strong all the time— because if you fall apart, everything else will, too.
- **The Ghost:** You stay quiet. You don't make waves. You try not to need too much—or anything at all.

Now ask yourself: Which of these roles feels most familiar? Where did you learn to play that role? What does it cost you to keep playing it?

You don't have to give up everything you've learned to do well. But if your role is costing you connection, authenticity, or peace—it might be time to shift.

Alignment doesn't mean you never play a role. It means you're no longer trapped in one.

KINDNESS AS CAMOUFLAGE

Debby's life was a masterclass in self-sacrifice. She gave and gave—meals, energy, emotional labor, time. She was the one people called when they needed casseroles, comfort, or crisis support—but never the one anyone asked, "How are you, really?" It wasn't just that she gave freely. She gave without limits. And when you give without limits, people rarely stop to ask what it's costing you.

In her world, boundaries were interpreted as rejection. Saying no meant you didn't care. Resting meant you weren't strong enough. Asking for space was treated like abandonment. So she internalized a story that love required self-erasure. Being needed was the same as being valued. The more she tolerated, the more lovable she believed she would be.

But what happens when kindness becomes a liability? When your generosity invites taking—but not giving in return? Debby wasn't just overextended—she was invisible. Not because no one saw her, but because she kept leaving herself out of the room.

Relational alignment isn't about baring it all or never serving others. It's about balance. Boundaries aren't about being cold—they're about being clear. They protect what we value and preserve what we need. They make relationships safer—not just for us, but for everyone involved.

Debby's version of vulnerability looked like endless giving. Like silence in the face of mistreatment. Like showing up to comfort people who never once asked how she was doing.

She armored up—not in a cold or distant way, but in a deeply conditioned, quietly suffocating way. She gave everything except her real self. Because that part? That part felt too risky to reveal.

NICE IS NOT THE SAME AS SAFE

Debby's story isn't unusual. I see it all the time—in different forms, with different costumes. And I hear the same advice given to people like her: "Just be more vulnerable." But vulnerability—true vulnerability—requires discernment. Not everyone can hold space for you. Not everyone should.

A safe person isn't someone who always agrees with you or makes you feel good. A safe person is someone who honors what you share. Who doesn't use your vulnerability against you. Who doesn't minimize your feelings, compete with your pain, or immediately make it about them.

A safe person listens without trying to fix. They don't disappear when things get messy. They're not perfect—but they're present. They show you, in small ways and over time, that you don't have to audition for their affirmation.

This doesn't mean you can only be vulnerable with people who meet some impossible standard. It just means you choose wisely. You reveal yourself at a pace that honors both your tenderness and your strength.

And here's the part that usually gets misunderstood—especially for people like Debby:

Self-love is not selfish. Selfishness says, "Only I matter." Self-love says, "I matter, too." Selfishness disregards impact. Self-love honors it. Selfishness grabs. Self-love grounds.

Boundaries aren't walls—they're windows with locks. They let people in—but only when it's safe. They give us the structure to choose how we show up, rather than reacting from fear or obligation.

Debby didn't need to stop loving people. She didn't need to stop caring. She just needed to learn that she was allowed to care for herself, too. That "kindness" without boundaries isn't noble—it's unsustainable. That her vulnerability was valuable, but only when it was protected by clarity and choice.

That's what relational alignment makes possible: not less connection, but truer connection. Not louder roles, but quieter honesty. Not performative loyalty, but care that flows both ways.

IT WAS EASIER TO GHOST ME THAN TO GROW

For a while, Debby pulled back. No big blow-up. No dramatic goodbye. Just a few missed sessions, a couple vague texts, and then silence. I wasn't surprised. The work we'd started—naming what she needed, getting honest about the cost of her roles—was uncomfortable. It's easier to ghost your therapist than to confess how hard the work is to do.

But after a few weeks, she came back. Quieter. Maybe a little embarrassed. But also, I think, ready to tell the truth.

The hardest part of setting boundaries isn't deciding where the line should be—it's managing what happens after you draw it. For people who've built their identity around being helpful, agreeable, or easy to love, even the gentlest boundary can feel like a betrayal.

Boundaries change the dynamic. They force clarity. And not everyone in your life will welcome that clarity.

You can't have alignment without vulnerability. But vulnerability without boundaries isn't brave. It's reckless. I tell clients: I could walk through the worst part of Cincinnati at 3 a.m., completely naked, holding a box full of cash. That would be incredibly vulnerable.

But it would also be incredibly dangerous.

When we offer parts of ourselves without filter, pacing, or trust, we aren't being courageous—we're setting ourselves up to be wounded.

Boundaries don't just protect your energy—they reveal your relationships. When you stop over-functioning, some people stop showing up. When you start asking for what you need instead of silently absorbing everything around you, some people get uncomfortable. And when you stop being the version of yourself that always says yes, you might realize some connections were built on usefulness—not intimacy.

That realization can be heartbreaking. You might grieve relationships you thought were deeper. Feel angry that people don't seem to want the real you—only the version who meets their needs. That grief is part of the process.

When boundaries and vulnerability work together, they create something truly liberating. You're no longer performing closeness—you're creating space for actual connection. You get to show up as you are and invite others to do the same.

HER FEET MATTER TOO

Debby's life was defined by care. On the surface, she cared for everyone. But when we looked more closely, most of her relationships were built around obligation, performance, or inherited patterns that had never been questioned. And the deeper we explored her relational world, the clearer it became: she didn't just struggle with boundaries—she didn't have room to consider what she actually wanted or needed.

Let's start with her marriage. Debby's husband was an alcoholic. He worked long hours, then came home and collapsed into the sofa like clockwork. He wasn't cruel, but he wasn't present either. She fed him. She brought him beers. She kept the house running so he wouldn't be disturbed. When we talked about her marriage, she never used words like intimacy, partnership, or trust. She said things like, "He works hard," or, "It's just easier if I take care of things." She had confused tolerance with love. That relationship wasn't mutual—it was mainte-nance. It functioned because Debby kept functioning.

Her relationship with her children was more tender. She adored them. She poured her entire self into making sure they had the emotional support and creative space she never had growing up. But even there, the lines were blurred. Her sense of purpose was so wrapped up in their well-being that she struggled when they didn't need her. As they got older, it got worse. She couldn't tolerate the teenage frustration or devel-opmental needs for independence because it made her feel unloved. And while her intentions were good, her role as a mother had become her entire identity.

Then there were her parents. Both were gone by the time she came to see me. Her grief wasn't sharp or raw—it was heavy, complicated, unre-solved. Her mother had also been married to an alcoholic. She raised Debby and her siblings while managing her own quiet despair. Debby admired her mother's strength but resented how she modeled silence as virtue. Her father, though often physically present, was emotionally absent. He didn't nurture, guide, or apologize. He existed in the house, and that was considered enough. After they died, Debby struggled to grieve. She wasn't mourning what she lost—she was mourning what she never had. And that kind of grief is sneaky. It doesn't show up at funerals. It shows up in therapy, years later, when you realize your emotional template was built on absence.

Her friendships weren't much better. She didn't have many, and the ones she did have leaned hard on her. She was the one who remembered birthdays, dropped off casseroles, and listened for hours without anyone asking about her own life. She didn't mind—or so she said. But over time, resentment crept in. It always does when relationships are one-way. She'd say things like, "They're just going through a lot," or, "They probably don't want to burden me." But what she meant was, "They don't see me." And more importantly, "I don't expect them to."

Even her relationship with her church was complicated. She'd grown up in a faith tradition that taught service, sacrifice, and submission as core values. She was always volunteering, always showing up early, always saying yes to the needs of others. But she felt lonely in that space. She never shared her personal struggles. She wasn't sure she'd be accepted if she stopped smiling. When she was exhausted, she stayed quiet. When she disagreed, she swallowed it. Her church offered community—but only as long as she stayed within the boundaries of what was considered acceptable. It was belonging with conditions.

She identified with the story of Jesus washing the apostles' feet—but for all the wrong reasons. To her, it wasn't a story about humility or sacred service. It was a blueprint for self-erasure. She didn't see the boundaries Jesus set elsewhere in his ministry, or the fact that he chose when and how to serve. She just saw the kneeling. The silence. The willingness to take on everyone else's dirt while asking nothing in return. That's what she thought love looked like. Not partnership. Not reciprocity. Just quiet, invisible sacrifice. She didn't see it as holy because it was chosen— she saw it as required. And that's what made it so dangerous.

But what that story was really about—in my opinion at least—was *choice*. Jesus didn't wash their feet because he was afraid they'd leave if he didn't. He wasn't trying to earn their affection or keep the peace. He did it to demonstrate love that was grounded in security, not fear. He knew who he was. He wasn't serving from emptiness—he was serving from abundance. And after he finished, he got up, put his robe back on, and continued the meal. That's not self-erasure. That's self-possession. It's the kind of love that bends down without losing itself in the process.

I challenged her gently one day. I said, "You find real joy in metaphorically washing other people's feet, right? In showing up, in serving, in caring?" She nodded. Of course she did. That part of her was sincere and beautiful.

"So then," I asked, "how dare you be so selfish... to deprive someone else of the joy of washing *yours*?"

She dismissed it—at first. Smiled. Changed the subject. But I could tell it landed. Maybe not all the way. But something had shifted.

Relational alignment requires us to re-evaluate the spaces we occupy— and the roles we've been handed or taken on. It's about looking at the people around us and asking not just, "Do I love them?" but, "Can I be myself with them?" It's about grieving the relationships that were never safe, even if they looked fine on paper. And it's about learning to show up differently—not because you're trying harder, but because you're finally showing up as you.

Debby used to think love meant kneeling at someone else's feet and staying there—quiet, useful, invisible. But toward the end of our work, she started standing. Not because she stopped loving, but because she started including herself in the equation. She still served. She still gave. But not as a way to disappear. Now, when she offers care, it's not a plea to be chosen—it's a choice she makes from a place of wholeness.

And sometimes, she even lets someone else care for her.

Not because she needs rescuing.

But because she finally knows her feet matter, too.

BELONGING WITHOUT DISAPPEARING

Debby didn't become a different person. But she started showing up in her life with a little more of herself in the room.

It began with small things. She stopped volunteering for everything at church. She skipped a women's event and didn't apologize for it. She let her voicemail pick up calls from friends who only ever wanted to vent. She deleted the Facebook birthday reminders and started reaching out only when it felt genuine—not obligatory.

With her kids, she let them solve more of their own problems. She began to untangle her sense of worth from their daily happiness. When one of them got frustrated with her and needed space, she didn't spiral. She let it be what it was, trusting the relationship to stretch instead of snap.

With her husband, things were harder. She didn't leave. But she started naming things—not every time, but sometimes. She said, "I feel invisible." She said, "I need help." And once, she said, "I don't want to be in this alone anymore."

He didn't magically transform, but something in her did. She stopped carrying the entire weight of the marriage on her back. She stopped assuming that survival was the same thing as success.

And in our work together, Debby stopped asking me how I was doing at the start of every session. She began showing up on time, sitting back instead of perching on the edge of the couch. She told stories about herself that didn't have a moral or a takeaway. She let herself be messy. She let herself be seen.

Healing didn't make her less kind. It just made her less available for the kind of connection that required her to disappear. And that's what relational alignment offers—not perfect relationships, but honest ones. Not an escape from discomfort, but a way to stay rooted inside yourself, even when things get hard.

She still had work to do. She still fell into old patterns sometimes. But she knew what it felt like to come home to herself.

And that feeling? That was new.

Debby's healing didn't happen all at once. It happened in a hundred tiny choices—what to say yes to, what to let go of, when to rest, and how to listen to herself again.

Because alignment isn't just about the big moments. It's about how we live when no one is watching.

SOUL AUDIT - RELATIONAL ALIGNMENT

Relational alignment is about showing up as your real self—not the version you think others can tolerate. It's about connection without contortion, and presence without performance.

Check all that apply:

- ☐ I often manage other people's emotions at the expense of my own
- ☐ I stay quiet to keep the peace, even when something matters to me
- ☐ I've realized some of my relationships leave me feeling smaller
- ☐ I'm not sure who truly loves me when I'm not trying to earn it
- ☐ **I'm starting to express my needs without guilt or apology**
- ☐ **I know what parts of me I've been shrinking to fit someone else**

You don't have to disappear to be loved. You don't have to audition to belong.

FROM THE AUDIT TO ACTION

AWARENESS

Some of the roles we play were handed to us early. Others we slipped into quietly over time. Either way, the longer we wear them, the harder they are to notice—until we try to take them off.

Ask yourself:

- *Who do I become around certain people?*
- *What role do I find myself performing most often—and why?*
- *What version of myself do I leave behind to keep certain relationships "easy"?*

PRACTICE

Try one of these micro-boundary experiments this week:

- *When someone asks for your time, pause. Instead of saying yes right away, say, "Let me check and get back to you."*
- *Let a text go unanswered for an hour. Or three.*
- *Practice naming a need out loud, even if it's small: "Actually, I need a quiet night."*
- *In a conversation, resist the urge to fix, perform, or pivot. Just show up honestly—even if you're tired.*
- *Ask a friend for something small—help, input, encouragement —just to practice being the one who receives.*

Realignment doesn't happen all at once. It starts with small, honest experiments in how you show up. Setting a boundary doesn't mean destroying everything.

But it does mean you have to stop destroying yourself for others.

CHAPTER 5
HURRY UP AND SLOW DOWN

NOT ALL MISALIGNMENT IS LIFE-ALTERING. Sometimes, it just shows up in your shoes.

One day, I spent an entire day—nine hours of back-to-back therapy sessions—with two different shoes on. Same style, but one was black and the other was brown. And I didn't notice. Not when I put them on. Not when I walked into my office. Not during intake questions or emotional breakthroughs. I crossed my legs, ushered clients from the lobby to the counseling room, nodded with empathy—all while wearing mismatched shoes.

It wasn't until my very last client of the day that anyone said a word. She looked down, then up at me, and asked—very casually—"Does that mean something?"

She wasn't joking. She genuinely thought it might be intentional. Like I was offering some kind of psychological Rorschach test. *Tell me how you feel about the shoes.* As if I were clever enough to make fashion a therapeutic metaphor.

I'm not that good.

I was misaligned all day—and had no idea. It wasn't a crisis but it took nine hours and one honest question to bring it into awareness.

That moment stuck with me—not because I was embarrassed (though I was), but because it perfectly captured how easily we drift into misalignment in daily life. We go through the motions. We show up. We check the boxes. And somewhere along the way, we stop noticing what we're carrying—or how it fits. Something feels off, but we don't question it because it still technically "works."

This chapter isn't about big identity shifts or dramatic breakdowns. It's about the little moments—the shoes, the coffee orders, the inbox, the calendar invites, the extra "sure" when we meant to say "no"—that quietly add up to the way we live.

Because soul alignment isn't just a concept. It's a practice. And it shows up in the tiniest of choices—especially when no one's watching.

Or when eight people are watching and just not saying anything.

TIME IS TELLING YOU SOMETHING

While I do enjoy a good sit, especially on vacation, I'm not someone who rests easily. I've had seasons where I was working multiple jobs, seeing clients, writing, speaking, performing, managing a business, and still showing up to support the people I care about. I've done more in a day than some people do in a week. That's not bragging—it's just reality.

So when I talk about time, I'm not talking about the kind of misalignment that comes from being aimless or unmotivated. I'm talking about the kind that sneaks up on people like me—the over-functioners. The helpers. The ones who say yes because we can. The ones who fill our calendars not because we're trying to prove something, but because we honestly believe it's what we're supposed to do.

And for a while, that works. We move fast. We get things done. People admire our work ethic. They tell us how dependable we are. And we start to believe that being available is the same thing as being valuable.

But eventually, the cracks show up.

We forget something important. We start snapping at people. We lose track of what matters—not because we don't care, but because there's no room left in our brains to hold anything that isn't urgent.

I've lived like that—overscheduled, overextended, overstimulated. Nothing catastrophic on the outside. But inside? I was resentful. Exhausted. Disconnected from myself. I was technically doing everything "right," but it didn't feel good. And when I finally stopped to look at my calendar, I realized something that shook me a little:

I didn't like the life I had created.

It was full of appointments, events, responsibilities, obligations. And most of them weren't inherently bad. They were things I said yes to reflexively—out of guilt, or pressure, or because I assumed no one else would step up.

But my time wasn't a reflection of my values. It was a reflection of my anxiety.

Time is honest. It will tell you exactly where you're aligned and exactly where you're not.

You say you want more rest, but you schedule meetings during your lunch hour. You say you want more joy, but you leave no space for it. You say you want deeper relationships, but your calendar is so full of obligations that you haven't had a real conversation in weeks. You say you want a life that feels meaningful, but you're chasing everyone else's emergencies instead.

None of that makes you a bad person. It just makes you someone who hasn't paused in a while to ask, "Is this mine?"

So if your life feels too fast, too noisy, or like it's running on autopilot—don't start with a to-do list. Start with your calendar. What's filling your time? What's draining it? What are you constantly rearranging your life around? What are you always too tired for?

Because time doesn't lie.

I don't need another productivity app. I don't need someone to teach me how to squeeze more into a day. What I need—what so many of us need—is to slow down long enough to ask if the way we're spending our time reflects the kind of life we actually want to live.

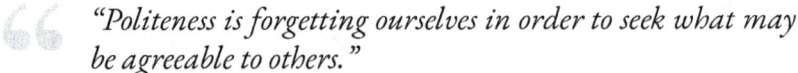

I LIKE TO BE LIKED

If time is one way we lose track of alignment, language is another.

It's amazing how many moments of micro-misalignment are hidden in politeness. The nod when you disagree. The smile when you're hurt. The "Sure, I'd be happy to," when every part of you wants to say no.

I know this one intimately. I've been a people-pleaser for most of my life. I don't like disappointing people. I enjoy being helpful. And I've been told I'm "nice"—which I used to think was the same thing as being good.

But it's not.

There's a quote I came across once that stuck with me:

> *"Politeness is forgetting ourselves in order to seek what may be agreeable to others."*

We call it "being kind," but if we're honest, sometimes it's just fear. Fear of being disliked. Fear of being misunderstood. Fear of taking up too much space.

Michael Scott from *The Office* once said, "I like to be liked. I enjoy being liked. I have to be liked. But it's not like this compulsive need to be liked, like my need to be praised." It's funny—because it's true. I laugh every time I watch it. And sometimes I wince, too. Because I get it.

We've been conditioned to be agreeable. But politeness without authenticity builds resentment. And resentment is relational rot.

So how do we break the pattern?

It starts with small acts of truth.

Check in:

Ask yourself: Am I saying yes because I want to or because it's expected?

Learn to pause. To feel. To notice when your yes comes from fear instead of desire.

And when you start setting boundaries—even with yourself—you must prepare for what follows: guilt, anxiety, the inner critic that whispers, "You're being selfish," or, "They're going to hate you," or, "You're not allowed to take up this much space."

That voice gets louder at first. But that doesn't mean it's right.

Politeness without honesty isn't kindness—it's strategy. It's self-preservation. And while there's nothing wrong with wanting to be kind, alignment asks a better question:

Is it costing you too much?

Because if it is, that's not kindness. That's a transaction.

And the more you trade your truth for someone else's comfort, the more invisible you become—to them and to yourself.

Alignment isn't about being rude. It's about being real. And sometimes, the kindest thing you can do for you and for the relationship is to tell the truth.

Even if it's just, "Actually, I'd rather not."

ARE THESE CHOICES EVEN MINE?

One of the reasons I love my Apple TV is that it offers me endless options. I fire it up and it shows me exactly where I left off on my latest binge, plus a dozen new things I might like based on my watch history. It's beautifully customized, and most of the time, I enjoy the experience of choosing.

But sometimes I'll open one of the twelve streaming services I subscribe to and spend forty minutes scrolling, weighing every possible option, reading episode descriptions, maybe watching a trailer—only to give up and go to bed. Too many choices become no choice at all.

I had a conversation recently about choice overload and decision fatigue, and it hit home. These are real psychological phenomena. Research shows that the more options we have, the more overwhelmed we become, and the more likely we are to either choose something we don't actually want—or avoid choosing altogether. And that's just Netflix. Multiply that energy by groceries, calendars, relationships, emails, outfits, and career paths, and suddenly your entire day starts to feel like a giant anxiety-inducing menu.

Choice is a foundational concept in counseling. In fact, one of the frameworks that has shaped my work is Choice Theory, developed by psychiatrist William Glasser in the 1960s. It teaches that we only have control over one person in life: ourselves. That's it. Not our spouses. Not our bosses. Not our kids or coworkers. Just us. Which means we are responsible for our choices—and also free to make different ones.

That might sound simple, but it's not easy. Because when we feel anxious, overwhelmed, or out of control, we often try to regain order by managing everything except ourselves. We set up elaborate routines, micromanage our environments, impose structure on chaos, and—without realizing it—try to control the feelings we're avoiding by controlling the world around us.

Mel Robbins writes about this in her book, *The Let Them Theory.* She explains that when people behave in ways you can't control, you don't have to chase, correct, or contort. You just let them. Let them flake. Let them misunderstand. Let them talk. It's not passivity—it's permission. Permission to stop managing what isn't yours, and to start paying attention to what is: your own response. Your own alignment. Your own next right choice.

I once worked with a psychologist who was one of the most anxious people I've ever met. On the surface, he looked composed—professional, well-spoken, always impeccably dressed. But the first thing I noticed? He tucked his sweater into his pants.

It wasn't a fashion choice. It was a signal. He was tightly wound, and so was his wardrobe. His day was ruled by routine. He followed the same exact schedule, drove the same route, packed the same lunch. And if anything disrupted that rhythm, it threw him into a tailspin. He didn't scream or panic—he just locked down even harder. For him, control was comfort.

When our inner world feels uncertain, we often double down on our outer world. And that can look like control, indecision, overcommitment, perfectionism, or endless scrolling on Apple TV.

So what does any of this have to do with alignment?

Everything.

Because alignment isn't about always knowing the right choice—it's about being conscious of your choices. It's about slowing down long enough to ask: *Does this feel like me? Is this decision rooted in clarity—or in fear?*

Alignment invites us to check in before we say yes. It asks us to notice what's driving our decision-making. Is it obligation? Guilt? Performance? Fear of missing out? The desire to be seen a certain way?

Or is it something deeper?

You don't have to overhaul your life to start living with intention. But you can begin by noticing how you respond to the hundreds of choices that cross your path every day. From the big ones—relationships, careers, commitments—to the small ones like what you wear or whether you say yes to one more thing when you're already tired.

We're making choices all the time—big ones, small ones, invisible ones. The real question is: Are they even ours?

SHOWING UP VS. GETTING THROUGH

My grandfather had style. His closet was packed—so full, in fact, that as he got older, he'd enlist my cousin and me to go through it and take home anything we could fit into. I like to think I inherited some of my fashion flair from him. There's just something about a good outfit that makes me feel more like myself.

Don't get me wrong—I love my Jedi-style bathrobe as much as anyone. It's enormous, soft, and comes complete with a hood. I've been known to float around my house like a dramatically cozy Luke Skywalker. But when I go out into the world? Sometimes, putting on a fun pair of glasses or a sharp shirt changes the whole tone of my day.

It's not really about fashion. It's about feeling.

When I'm dressed in a way that reflects how I want to show up, I feel more confident. More grounded. More whole.

And when I'm not? I notice.

I think back to the day I wore two different shoes—or to the anxious psychologist with the tucked-in sweater. Tiny wardrobe choices, yes—but also quiet clues that something was off.

What we wear can be one of the simplest and clearest forms of self-expression. But it can also become armor. For some people, dressing down is a signal to stay invisible. For others, dressing up is a way to feel worthy enough to be seen. That kid in the hoodie who sits quietly in the corner? That woman who always and only wears black?

None of it is wrong. But perhaps it deserves our curiosity.

Sometimes, when we feel out of control emotionally, we try to correct it physically. We clean the house, organize a drawer, over-accessorize. Or we stop trying altogether. We stay in pajamas for days and call it "comfort" when what we really feel is numb. There's no shame in any of that —but there's information.

That's what alignment invites us to notice: What am I trying to say with this choice? And is it honest?

Some days, I feel most myself in a t-shirt and jeans. Other days, I want a bright shirt and statement shoes. I've learned that what I put on my body affects what I access in my soul—not because clothes are magic, but because attention is.

Depression researchers often recommend getting dressed and taking a shower as part of a treatment plan—not because it fixes anything, but because it creates movement. A small, tangible reminder that you still exist. That you're still in there.

And sometimes, when we don't know where to start, a hot shower and clean socks can be the first brave step back toward ourselves.

So ask yourself: What do you feel best in? What makes you feel most like you?

And when you look in the mirror, do you see someone showing up... or someone just getting through?

Alignment doesn't only show up in the big stuff. It's not reserved for identity crises, career shifts, or dramatic revelations. It's in the socks. The scrolls. The way we move through our day when no one else is watching.

SOUL AUDIT: DAILY ALIGNMENT

Your time isn't just how you spend your hours—it's how you spend your life. And life alignment often shows up in small, ordinary choices.

Check all that apply:

- ☐ I feel like I'm always rushing—even when I have nowhere urgent to be
- ☐ I say yes out of habit, not desire
- ☐ I regularly prioritize productivity over presence
- ☐ I rarely stop to ask how I'm actually feeling before making decisions
- ☐ **I've made at least one small change that's helped me feel more like myself**
- ☐ **I can tell when my pace is serving me—and when it's not**

You don't have to overhaul your schedule to reclaim your alignment. But you might need to pause. Notice what your pace is doing to your presence—and whether the life you're building still feels like yours.

FROM THE AUDIT TO ACTION

Awareness

Most misalignment doesn't start with a crisis. It starts with a habit. A scroll. A sigh. A silent yes. A pair of shoes that don't match and no one says a word.

Ask yourself:

- *When do I feel most on autopilot?*
- *Where do I default to politeness over honesty?*
- *What's one area of my life that works technically—but doesn't feel good anymore?*
- *What's my most frequent "almost no" that turns into a "sure"?*

Small misalignments are still misalignments. And they're often the easiest place to begin real change.

Practice

This week, try this:

- *Pick one ordinary part of your life—what you wear, how you spend your lunch break, your evening wind down—and make a small, conscious change:*
- *Choose clothes that make you feel you*
- *Say no to one thing that's "just fine"*
- *Pause before you reflexively open an app*
- *Set a boundary around your time—even if it's just for 20 minutes*

You don't need a massive overhaul. You need five minutes of truth.

Alignment isn't about overhauling your entire life. It's about making tiny choices that tell the truth about who you are.

CHAPTER 6
GOD DOESN'T NEED YOU TO AUDITION

I USED to think the sacred only showed up in certain places, with certain people, in certain ways.

Holiness was something you performed—on Sunday mornings, under lights, with hands raised and a worship leader telling you when to feel something. I knew the script. I even liked the script. But I've been wondering lately if that version of spirituality ever really aligned with who I was.

A few months ago, I hosted a small gathering to celebrate the release of *Jesus & Me* and *The Search Party*, my debut novel. It wasn't a launch party, exactly—just an evening of music, poetry, and reflection in my friend Sharon's living room. A handful of folding chairs, a few friends, and a gorgeous grand piano. No stained glass. No altar. No hymnal in sight. Just people.

Honestly? It felt more spiritual than many church services I've attended.

It wasn't overly produced. (OK, I'm me—so it was *lightly* produced. But it was in a living room. So . . .) I figured I'd read some things, let my musical theatre friends sing a couple of songs, and we'd call it a night.

But then something happened.

After the last planned piece, LaShanda stepped forward. She wasn't scheduled to share. She hadn't even planned to come until earlier that week. But there she was offering something so unvarnished it shifted the energy in the room. She talked about the impact I'd had on her and others. It was validating and kind and unexpected.

Then Sharon spoke. Then Cheryl. It was lovely.

Afterwards, we sat and talked. Caught up with old friends. Shared time and ourselves. And something about that moment felt holy.

Not in the way I used to think of holy—not polished or dramatic or emotionally manipulative. Just... set apart. Quiet. Alive. Like something deeper had shown up and taken a seat with us.

I don't know what to call it exactly. But I know what it wasn't.

It wasn't pretend.

THE HOLY WHISPER

And the wildest part? LaShanda wasn't even supposed to be there.

A few months earlier, I'd commented on something she posted on Facebook. We've always had a strange kind of connection—on paper, we don't seem alike. But we both love pro wrestling. We're both therapists who self-disclose publicly, walking the razor's edge between transparency and privacy.

And... we're both a little psychic.

I had a hunch something was off, so I messaged her: "Are you okay?"

She could have said "I'm fine." But she didn't. She told the truth. And I offered what I could: presence, affirmation, specificity. Not a pep talk. Just real connection. And then life went on.

But the week of the concert, LaShanda emailed me out of the blue. Just said I'd been on her mind. She didn't know about the event. She hadn't seen the social media posts about it. Sharon hadn't talked to her in a minute. But she came. Because something nudged her. Something whispered, "Reach out."

Call it what you want. Coincidence. Intuition. Energy. Spirit.

All I know is: I couldn't have planned it. And I wouldn't trade it for anything.

WHAT COUNTS

I've spent a lot of my life trying to figure out what "counts" as spiritual. I grew up with a version that was very specific—certain language, certain postures, certain rules. And while some of those things still hold meaning for me, I've come to believe that spirituality is bigger than any one tradition. It's not about where you go on Sundays or how many Bible verses you've memorized. It's not about burning sage or manifesting or finding the perfect meditation app.

Spiritual alignment isn't about *looking* spiritual. It's about feeling connected—to yourself, to others, to something greater. To meaning. To movement. To mystery.

For some people, that connection still lives in the church. For others, it's found in nature, art, stillness, or unexpected moments in living rooms.

You don't have to go to church—or walk away from one, either—to find spiritual alignment. It doesn't ask you to adopt a label, a ritual, or a particular vocabulary. But if you do find comfort in a faith tradition, alignment means your values and beliefs should resonate with what that tradition teaches. If you're constantly explaining away or excusing harm in the name of community, that's not alignment. That's spiritual dissonance. But you can love Jesus and walk away from churches that don't reflect his teachings. You can stay in your faith and still ask hard questions. What matters most is that your soul isn't living in fear of the very thing that's supposed to bring you peace.

It's about noticing when your soul lights up—and when it shuts down. It's about paying attention to what restores you—and what wears you down. It's about unlearning the idea that spirituality is a performance, and relearning what it means to simply be aligned.

(If you want the deeper dive on my own spiritual story—including what I used to believe, what I still hold, and what I've let go of—I wrote a whole book about it. It's called *Jesus & Me,* and it traces that winding path in much more detail than I can do here. This chapter isn't meant to retell that story, but to hold space for all of ours.)

THE CLIENT WHO DIDN'T NEED ME TO KNOW

Not every moment of spiritual alignment comes from shared understanding. Sometimes, it begins with being willing to sit in the mystery—especially when the tradition in question isn't your own.

I once worked with a client—we'll call her Mariam—who was raised in a conservative Muslim household. She was kind, curious, and sharp as hell. And from the beginning, she was clear: she wasn't coming to therapy to deconstruct her religion. She still found beauty in parts of her faith. The cadence of the prayers. The collective fasting during Ramadan. The language her grandmother used when she blessed her forehead.

But there were parts that no longer felt like hers.

Mariam had spent years trying to reconcile her identity as a modern, ambitious woman with teachings that—at least in her interpretation—asked her to be smaller. Quieter. Less visible. Less opinionated. Less free.

She told me, "I used to think I was failing my faith. But now I think maybe the version I was taught just doesn't fit anymore."

I didn't pretend to be an expert on Islam. I told her as much. In fact, I told her I was worried I'd mess something up. Say the wrong thing. Assume too much. But Mariam smiled.

"That's why I picked you," she said. "I don't need you to know everything about my religion. I just need you to help me trust what I already know."

She wasn't asking me for answers. She was asking me to hold space while she honored what still felt sacred—and gently released what didn't.

Her story reminded me that spiritual alignment isn't about choosing the right tradition or finding the perfect label. It's about resonance. Honesty. The ability to say, "This no longer fits," without fear of exile. And to say, "This still matters," even if no one else understands why.

Mariam didn't leave her faith entirely. But she stopped twisting herself to match a mold that no longer reflected who she was. She stopped trying to earn love by disappearing. She stopped apologizing for her questions.

And in that quiet, steady unfolding, something sacred emerged.

Not certainty. But peace.

Soul Audit: Spiritual Alignment

Spiritual alignment isn't about dogma or performance. It's about resonance—when your soul knows it's home, even if it can't explain why.

Check all that apply:

- ☐ I've felt pressure to prove my worth in spiritual or religious spaces
- ☐ **I've questioned beliefs I used to accept without hesitation**

- ☐ I've experienced moments that felt sacred—without being "religious"
- ☐ I'm learning to trust my own inner knowing, even when it's inconvenient
- ☐ I can name practices or moments that help me feel connected to something bigger
- ☐ I've let go of trying to impress God (or the universe, or anyone else)

There's no score here—just patterns to notice. If some of these statements felt true for you, you're doing well. Spiritual alignment looks different for everyone, but it often begins with honesty. The more we pay attention to what brings us peace, clarity, and connection—and what doesn't—the more clearly we can hear the voice beneath the noise.

FROM THE AUDIT TO ACTION

Awareness

You don't have to abandon your faith to find alignment. But you do have to tell the truth about how it's been shaping—or distorting—your soul.

Ask yourself:

- *Where do I feel most spiritually alive—and where do I go numb?*
- *What parts of my spiritual identity were inherited, not chosen?*
- *What does my soul know is true, even if I don't have words for it yet?*
- *Where am I still performing in order to be seen as "good," "worthy," or "faithful"?*

Spiritual alignment doesn't demand certainty. It invites honesty.

PRACTICE

This week, try one small act of spiritual realignment:

- *Return to a place that makes you feel connected (a trail, a song, a theatre seat, a notebook)*
- *Name a belief you've outgrown—even if just in your journal*
- *Let yourself pray, or meditate, or cry—or laugh—without trying to explain it*
- *Say, "I don't know what I believe about that"—and notice what that loosens in you*

You don't need to audition for meaning. You're already enough. And the holy thing is often the honest thing.

CHAPTER 7
THE GOSPEL ACCORDING TO MERYL

In the last chapter, we talked about presence—the kind that doesn't need polish or performance.

This chapter asks a deeper version of the same question:

Where does your spirit feel most present? Most alive? Most at home?

While I shared how that presence showed up in unexpected places—like a living room gathering—for me, it's also shown up in another unexpected sanctuary: the theatre.

Theatre didn't just give me a stage. It gave me a new framework for what it meant to be real.

I started out as an audience member—watching, absorbing, letting other people's stories move me. Later, I became a critic, trying to capture what worked and what didn't, what felt true and what felt forced. Eventually, I began writing plays myself, learning how to shape a story from the inside out. I even acted a time or two—enough to know how vulnerable it is to stand in someone else's shoes and tell the truth out loud.

It's where I learned one of the most important lessons about alignment: good acting isn't good *pretending*. Good acting requires telling the *truth*.

That's the simplest way I know how to explain it. The difference between pretending and presence is honesty. And whether I'm watching a performance or sitting across from a client, I can feel it when someone's not fully in the room.

In therapy, we call that congruence—the alignment between what someone says and what their body, tone, and energy are doing. A client might tell me they're "fine" while their foot taps furiously and their eyes won't meet mine. Something's not lining up.

The same thing happens onstage. A line can be delivered perfectly, with excellent diction and timing, and still fall flat if it isn't coming from someplace real.

Growing up, I led worship at my hometown church. I knew how to create a moment: show up early, set up the sound system, rehearse, perform. I could sell a song, strike the right emotional tone, even write original music for a sermon series. But while I was offering parts of myself on the surface, I was hiding more underneath. I was still closeted. Still afraid that if people knew who I really was, everything I offered would be disqualified. That fear didn't disappear just because I could belt out a glory note.

I wasn't leading worship to live my truth—I was performing to belong. For validation. And to stay connected to a faith that felt like it might spit me out if it knew the whole story.

Pretending is surface-level. It's self-protective. We pretend to believe. To be confident. To be healed. But the performance is brittle. It cracks when we're alone, or when someone asks the right question, or when anxiety hits harder than usual and there's no script for that.

Good acting—the kind that moves you—is the opposite of fake. It's rooted in deep listening. The best actors aren't the ones who memorize best—they're the ones who stay open. Who let the moment shape them. Who don't push or posture or try to control the scene—they just show up and tell the truth.

That's the kind of spirituality I want.

Not a religion of pretense. Not a mask I wear to fit in. But a lived faith that invites presence. That demands congruence. That lets me show up as I am—doubts, scars, weird quirks and all—and still be met with grace. Maybe even still be useful.

I've learned to spot pretense quickly. In church. In therapy. In relationships. I don't have much tolerance for it anymore—not because I'm above it, but because I've spent too many years doing it myself. And it never gave me what I was looking for.

Pretending is exhausting. But acting—when it's honest—is exhilarating.

And if you want to see what that kind of alignment looks like in real time?

Watch Meryl Streep.

She doesn't just act—she listens. Not in a "look what I can do" way, but in a deeply empathetic, almost reverent way. Every character she plays feels specific, human, alive. She never pushes. She never fakes. She enters the truth of the moment and makes herself available to it.

That's what makes her the best actress of all time, in my opinion. Not the accents or the awards. It's that she never loses herself—but she also never insists on herself. She becomes a vessel for something true.

She once said, "Empathy is at the heart of the actor's art. It's the current that connects you to the other soul."

That is spiritual.

And maybe that's what I'm after in my own spiritual life—not certainty, not performance, but that same kind of open-hearted presence. That Meryl Streep spirituality. The kind that says, "Let me tell the truth, even if it's hard."

SOFAS, SCRIPTS, AND STAYING QUIET

Performance isn't limited to the stage and screen.

I see it in therapy all the time. People walk in hoping to be helped—but also hoping to be seen a certain way. They want to be the "good client." They want to have the right insights, the right words, the story that makes sense. Sometimes they want to convince me of something they don't even believe themselves: that they're healed. That they're over it. That they're fine.

We all do this. We curate. We perform. We pretend we're not hurting or scared or furious with God. We pray the "right" way. We say the lines we've heard others say before us. We assume belonging is awarded to those who hit their marks and stay in character.

But real transformation doesn't happen when we're pretending. It happens when we get honest.

It happens when we drop the script and say the actual thing. When we stop trying to impress and start trying to connect. When we admit, "I'm terrified," or "I don't know what I believe anymore," or "I'm furious at the silence," or "I need to be held."

And here's where it gets wild:

God—or the Universe or whomever you believe is out there—doesn't need us to get into character. The divine doesn't respond to costume changes or perfect lighting cues. The invitation is to show up as we are —unscripted, unpolished, undone—and still belong.

So what if your spiritual life is less about playing the part—and more about inhabiting the scene you're in fully? No pretense. No applause. Just the courage to be real. But being real isn't always loud or brave or dramatic. Sometimes it's just a quiet decision in a hallway, in your living room, in your own head:

Do I speak up, or do I keep pretending I'm fine?

But not all pretending looks dramatic. Sometimes, it's quieter than that. Sometimes, the performance isn't what we say   it's what we *don't* say.

The silence we keep to avoid disruption. The smile we offer when something feels off. The nod we give instead of asking a question.

That's still a kind of pretending. A way we perform safety instead of pursuing truth.

Take, for example, a sofa.

I'd bought a blue leather one with power everything. It was on sale and I was so proud of the deal I'd gotten. When the delivery guys arrived, they seemed confident. I figured they knew what they were doing—so I didn't say anything, even though something about the wrapping looked... off.

They hauled the thing up the steps, maneuvered it through a tight turn, and placed it in my living room. It wasn't until I mentioned the deal I'd gotten—specifically on the leather and power features—that they stopped.

One looked at the other. Then at me.

"We brought the wrong one up."

Turns out it wasn't leather. Or blue. Or mine.

"He's so mad at me," the lead said, motioning to his partner. "If I weren't saved, I'd probably choke him," the other joked. We all laughed. Thankfully.

I'd wondered about it back at the truck, but figured they knew what they were doing. I shrugged and said, "I'm usually pretty bossy, but I'm working on that. So I didn't ask any questions."

That wasn't the first time I stayed quiet to keep the peace.

Once, I had a massage from a guy who wouldn't stop talking. I learned about his daughter, his previous therapist, his medications, his daughter's softball games, his career history, and his divorce. At one point he said, "If I'm talking too much, just let me know."

I said, "Oh, it's fine."

But it wasn't.

Later, I told a friend. She said, "But you're so assertive! Why didn't you just tell him to stop?"

I guess I'm less assertive when I'm half-naked under a sheet.

The delivery guys sighed, took the giant wrong couch back downstairs, then brought the right one up. I tipped them more than I'd planned. I gave them bottled water. I wished them well.

And then I sat there replaying what I should have said.

I could have asked, "That doesn't look like mine—are you sure?"

I could have said, "Just to double-check, it's the blue leather one, right?"

I could have trusted my gut and spoken up.

But I didn't.

And that moment reminded me: Silence isn't always kindness.

THE COUCH WAS NEVER THE POINT

Maybe it wasn't about a couch at all.

Maybe it was about how often we lose our voices in small, ordinary moments—how we pretend we're fine when we're not.

Often we try to "go with the flow" when something in us is screaming, *Say something.* Maybe we're all still learning the difference between silence and surrender, aggression and authenticity, acting and pretending.

But here's the spiritual part:

When I ignore my voice—when I defer, shrink, avoid, or pretend—I disconnect from the person I was made to be.

When I override my instincts to keep the peace, to avoid embarrassment, to stay in control, I'm not just avoiding conflict—

I'm avoiding presence.

And presence is where Spirit lives.

Spiritual alignment, at its core, isn't about belief or ritual or performance. It's about being honest in real time. It's about listening inward and responding outward with integrity. It's about showing up fully in the moment—even if that moment is weird or tense or completely out of your control.

That's why pretending is so dangerous—not just emotionally, but spiritually. Because pretending keeps us outside ourselves. It keeps us polished but unrooted. The sacred can't reach us when we're covered in armor.

That's the spiritual lesson of the couch: Not just that I should've spoken up about furniture. But that I get to choose—every moment—whether I want to be in control, or in communion.

Control means managing how I'm perceived, staying comfortable, and avoiding risk.

Communion means showing up honestly, allowing myself to be seen, and trusting that connection is possible—even if the moment is awkward, inconvenient, or imperfect.

It's the difference between keeping things tidy and letting them be true.

I don't think the sacred shows up in our most polished impressions of who we think we should be. I think it meets us in the honest moment we stop performing and start paying attention. Even if that moment involves two delivery guys and a spiral of internal monologue that could rival a Shakespearean soliloquy.

SOUL AUDIT: PRESENCE & PRETENDING

You don't need to be polished to be present. Alignment isn't about impressing anyone—it's about being honest, even when it's inconvenient.

Check all that apply:

- ☐ I often catch myself performing without realizing it
- ☐ I've stayed silent to protect a version of me someone else expects
- ☐ **I can tell when something sounds right but doesn't feel true**
- ☐ **I've found places where I don't have to edit myself**
- ☐ **I'm beginning to trust that I don't have to earn belonging**
- ☐ **I've started saying out loud things I used to only rehearse in my head**

Pretending doesn't always mean lying. Sometimes, it's just staying quiet when something true wants to be spoken. Sometimes, it's offering a smile when you really need to set a boundary.

Presence begins when you stop performing and start being.

FROM THE AUDIT TO ACTION

Awareness

Performance can be sneaky. It doesn't always come with a spotlight or applause. Sometimes it sounds like, *"I'm fine."* Sometimes it looks like silence. Or shrinking. Or smiling when you want to scream.

Ask yourself:

- *Where am I working harder to be liked than to be honest?*
- *Where do I stay quiet when my gut says, "Say something"?*
- *When do I trade truth for smoothness—and what does that cost me?*
- *What's one space where I could stop performing and just be?*

Presence begins when you stop auditioning and start arriving.

PRACTICE

This week, pause in one small moment—a text, a comment, a choice—and ask yourself:

- *"Am I performing right now? Or am I present?"*
- *If the answer is performing, don't panic. Just choose again:*
- *Say one small truth: "Actually, I don't love that idea."*
- *Ask for what you need: "Can we slow down for a sec?"*
- *Share something real: "This is hard to say, but here's the truth..."*

You don't have to be dramatic. Just honest. Just here. Pretending is about control. Presence is about connection.

Choose connection.

CHAPTER 8
NO IS A SACRED WORD

He showed up looking like hell.

Hair unwashed, sweatshirt inside-out, eyes ringed with the kind of purple only deep exhaustion can pull off. He slumped into the chair across from me, and before I could even ask how he was, he said, "I think my dog and I are trauma-bonded."

I raised an eyebrow, and he half-laughed. "No, seriously. He panics when I leave. He howls and shuts down. And I—I don't howl, but I get it. I get that freeze. The fear. The needing everything to feel controlled."

His name was Zach. Thirty-five. Nonprofit worker by day, caregiver by default. Everyone leaned on him. He never leaned back.

"I'm tired, man," he said. "Like, sick tired. My apartment smells like a vet's office, my dog has psychological problems, I haven't done laundry in two weeks, and I just... I don't know. I feel behind in my own life."

We sat with that for a minute. I didn't rush in with a question. I've learned sometimes silence is the best tool in my box.

Eventually he said, "I don't even think I'm depressed. I think I'm just... doing everything for everyone all the time. And my body's like, 'Cool, we're done now.'"

He wasn't wrong. His exhaustion didn't sound like collapse—it sounded like misalignment. Like too many "yeses" layered on top of each other. Like a soul that hadn't had space to say what it actually needed.

And when we traced it back, it didn't start with the dog. It didn't start with his job. It started years ago, when saying "no" wasn't an option.

Zach grew up in a house where love wasn't language—it was labor. If you wanted to be wanted, you made yourself useful. If you had a need, you kept it small. If you had a boundary, you swallowed it.

He was the sensitive kid. The responsible one. The emotional translator in a household that never said the words. And over time, his usefulness became his identity.

"I know people love me," he told me. "Like, logically, I know that. But it's like my brain disqualifies it. I keep thinking, 'Why would anyone choose to love *me*?'"

That's what happens when your early life teaches you that love is conditional. You start to believe that your worth is performance-based. That your needs are too much. That your "no" is a threat.

That's not selfishness. That's survival.

But here's the thing about survival strategies: they work until they don't.

Soul alignment means telling the truth—not just to yourself, but in the way you *live*. It means your schedule reflects your values. Your voice reflects your boundaries. Your relationships reflect mutuality.

But you can't live aligned if you're constantly overextending to stay safe.

Zach wasn't saying yes because he wanted to. He was saying yes because he didn't know he *could* say no. Because "no" still felt like rejection. Like failure. Like letting someone down.

And here's what I told him: You don't have to collapse to earn rest.

You don't have to explain your no with a 12-slide PowerPoint. You don't have to wait until you're sleep-deprived and emotionally brittle to say, "That doesn't work for me."

Alignment doesn't always feel comfortable. Especially not at first. Especially if you've spent your life proving, pleasing, or managing other people's reactions.

But discomfort isn't danger. And boundaries aren't barriers—they're declarations of dignity.

We worked together for several more weeks. Nothing dramatic happened. Zach didn't quit his job or ghost his friends or become a No Man. But little things shifted.

He paused before saying yes. He noticed when his body tightened. He canceled a dinner he didn't want to go to and didn't apologize for it. He took a nap in the middle of a Saturday—just because he wanted to. And in one of our last sessions, he said:

 "I think I'm learning that love doesn't have to be earned. And that rest doesn't have to be justified. That maybe—maybe—I can say no and still be a good person."

That, to me, is what alignment looks like in real life. Quiet. Honest. No longer negotiable. It's not a mountaintop epiphany. It's a quiet "no" that you don't flinch while saying. It's the sacred pause between the question and your answer—the moment you ask, *what's true for me right now?*

I HATE EGGS

Boundary work doesn't always show up in big, dramatic ways. Sometimes it sneaks up on you at breakfast.

A few years ago, I found myself staying at a Bed and Breakfast. That alone was out of character—I usually prefer hotels for the anonymity and the lack of required small talk. At a hotel, I can just exist. At a Bed and Breakfast, I feel like I've wandered into someone's home and now I'm expected to bond with them over orange juice and doilies. But I was visiting friends who were performing at a small amusement park in rural Pennsylvania, and hotel options were limited. So I booked a charming little B&B that promised a private bathroom and Wi-Fi—my two minimum standards for surviving quaintness.

The room was fine—very blue, very floral, very much like something my mother would've decorated in 1993. I slept well enough, and in the morning I wandered into the kitchen, where the innkeeper greeted me warmly and told me, with great enthusiasm, that she could make me any kind of eggs I wanted. She had English muffins, fresh juice, and was especially proud of her omelets.

I hate eggs. Hate them. Scrambled eggs look like yellow-flavored vomit. Over easy is just an unborn chicken on a plate. And omelets? A crime against texture. But instead of telling her any of that, I panicked.

"Um... an omelet with ham sounds great," I said.

My logic, if you could call it that, was that I could scrape the ham out of the egg casing and salvage my breakfast without offending my host. But the ham had been thoroughly "eggified," and I have a powerful gag reflex when it comes to food that disgusts me. There's no poker face. My body reacts. Visibly.

So there I sat, making polite conversation with the innkeeper and her husband, asking them about how they ended up running a B&B while trying to discreetly rearrange the contents of my plate so it looked like I had eaten most of it. I smiled. I nodded. I mashed up the evidence. Then I got in my car, drove five minutes down the road, and ordered a bacon and cheese biscuit from McDonald's—*no egg, of course.*

It was just a breakfast. But it left me thinking about all the ways I say yes when I don't mean it. About how often I've swallowed something I didn't want—literally or figuratively—just to avoid disappointing some-one. Just to keep the peace. Just to seem polite.

That's the thing about misalignment: it doesn't always show up in crisis. Sometimes it's in the smallest choices. The quietest moments. The plate of food you didn't ask for but felt obligated to eat.

And every time we override our instincts to make someone else more comfortable, we teach ourselves that our needs are negotiable.

It's not about the eggs. It's about the cost of being agreeable.

TIRED OF EVERYTHING

A few years ago, I got *volun-told* to speak at a summer program for a group of high school students participating in a vocational initiative. The idea was to give them a mental health presentation—something about depression, self-care, that sort of thing. I was told I'd be repeating the presentation several times throughout the day for rotating groups.

What I wasn't told—at least not clearly—was that these kids weren't there by choice. They hadn't opted in. They were in the program because someone told them they had to be. And they weren't interested in a lecture from a therapist. They were tired. Hot. Hungry. Over it before it even began.

I stood up in front of the first group with my best "I'm here to help" smile, and it was pure hell. Most of the kids talked through it. Some were openly dismissive. A few laughed. One kid threw something across the room. It was chaos, and I had no real support to redirect or manage any of it.

At one point, I just sat down, crossed my arms, and gave up. I didn't yell. I didn't leave. I just... stopped.

There was a young woman in the front row—kind, quiet, trying to listen—who leaned forward like she was trying to comfort me. And that moment broke my heart more than the disrespect. Because it wasn't her job to make *me* feel safe. She was a teenager. I was the adult. But in that moment, I didn't feel like I had anything left to give.

When it was over, I swore I'd never go back.

But the next summer? They asked again. Said it would be different. Promised there'd be more support. Said the students would be better prepared. That it wouldn't be like last time.

And this time, I said no.

Not because I was bitter. Not because I didn't believe in the mission. But because it didn't feel safe. It wasn't healthy for me. And honestly? It wasn't worth the cost to my soul.

They asked again. Tried to pressure me. I stood my ground. I was ready to quit my job if I had to. I didn't go back. I meant what I said.

There are some things that just aren't worth it.

And sometimes, alignment means knowing that *early* and saying so *clearly*.

Soul alignment doesn't live in your intentions. It lives in your behavior.

You can believe all the right things—about boundaries, rest, your own worth—but if you keep putting yourself in situations that drain and deplete you, then your soul never actually gets to feel the benefit of what you believe.

Your "no" is part of your self-care practice. Not because it's defiant. But because it's *true*.

I thought about that moment with the summer program when I sat across from Zach, who slumped into my office with that look people get when they've said yes too many times in a row.

"I'm not depressed," he said. "I'm just so tired. Of everything."

Zach wasn't in crisis. He hadn't lost anything major. He wasn't newly grieving or freshly traumatized. He was just quietly burnt out.

The kind of burnout that sneaks up on people who don't give themselves permission to stop.

"I feel like I've created a version of myself that everyone expects to show up," he told me. *"And if I stop doing, I don't know who I am."*

This is what happens when your "yes" becomes a survival strategy.

You forget that you ever had the right to say no.

Zach didn't hate his job. He wasn't trying to escape his relationships. He just didn't know how to set a boundary without feeling like he was letting someone down.

Zach isn't the only one who's learned that lie. A lot of us have.

Especially if we grew up in family systems that prized self-sacrifice over self-awareness or workplaces that reward burnout and call it excellence. We are trained to believe that over-functioning is noble. That saying yes is generous. That being agreeable is moral.

But here's the truth:

You aren't aligned if your yes is dishonest.

If you're saying yes from fear—of conflict, of rejection, of being seen as difficult—it's not a real yes. It's just a performance. And soul alignment doesn't ask for performance. It asks for presence. It asks for truth.

Zach eventually did say no. To something small. A group dinner he didn't want to attend. He texted me later to say he stayed home, took a long bath, and watched a movie by himself for the first time in months.

"I didn't even feel guilty," he said. "Just... relieved."

That's when I knew he was on the path—not just to better boundaries, but to wholeness. Because when you stop abandoning yourself to keep the peace, that's not selfishness. That's healing.

SOUL AUDIT: BOUNDARIES & BELONGING

Boundaries aren't rude. They're how we stop abandoning ourselves in the name of keeping the peace.

Check all that apply:

- ☐ I say yes more out of guilt than desire
- ☐ I struggle to rest unless I've "earned it"
- ☐ I shrink my needs to avoid conflict or rejection
- ☐ I know what no feels like in my body, but don't always honor it
- ☐ **I've begun setting boundaries that reflect my worth— not just my limits**
- ☐ **I'm learning that saying no doesn't make me mean—it makes me honest**

Boundary work is rarely about pushing people away. It's about calling yourself back.

Your "no" isn't a rejection. It's a reclamation of your energy. Your time. Your truth.

FROM THE AUDIT TO ACTION

Awareness

Boundaries aren't just walls—they're agreements with yourself about where your energy, time, and tenderness are safe to give.

Start here:

- *Notice where you leave conversations feeling smaller, not bigger.*
- *Notice when a "yes" leaves a bad taste in your mouth.*

- *Notice where you feel like you're giving pieces of yourself away without truly choosing to.*

These aren't failures. They're invitations.

PRACTICE

Pick one place this week where you often overextend yourself without even realizing it.

(Think: staying on a call too long, picking up extra work, absorbing someone else's emotions.)

Choose one moment to pause before responding.

Ask yourself: *"Am I offering this—or am I surrendering it?"*

A healthy boundary isn't about rejecting people.

It's about honoring your own dignity while staying connected.

CHAPTER 9
THE VOICE IN MY HEAD ISN'T EVEN MINE

In first grade Sunday school, my teacher said—casually but confidently—that if we didn't close our eyes while we prayed, our prayers wouldn't count. I never forgot it.

I have closed my eyes every single time I prayed after that. Not because it feels sacred or because I'm overcome with reverence. I do it because I'm afraid not to. Because somewhere in me, a seven-year-old is still terrified that if I don't get it exactly right, God won't hear me. The prayer won't count. And I'll be the one who ruined it.

I wonder... what else was I taught that's stuck somewhere in my psyche?

That kind of shame is hard to unlearn. It's quiet, not dramatic. It doesn't come with flashing lights or trauma headlines. But it lives in the body. It lives in small rituals and hesitations. It hides behind politeness and perfectionism and doing things "the right way," even when you're not sure what that means anymore.

The older I get, the more I realize how much of my life has been shaped by voices that weren't actually mine. Teachers. Pastors. Parents. Supervisors. Critics. I've internalized so many scripts about who I'm supposed to be and how I should show up. And when I don't meet those expectations—or even think I might have—I feel it.

Even now, I still panic a little when someone says, "Can we talk?" without telling me what it's about. I imagine the worst. I brace for impact. It's the same with canceled client appointments that don't come with a reason. With surprise emails from my landlord. With notes taped to my door. Some small, protective part of me assumes I've done something wrong. That I'm in trouble. That I've failed.

Sometimes, I even catch myself assuming that things like this book won't be well received because people can sense that I didn't quite earn it. Or that a reader hated it because they haven't left a review. Or that I should've worked harder, edited more, gotten it "more right."

I can't always tell the difference between responsibility and shame. I'm still learning.

When I released *The Search Party*, the first print run was riddled with typos. I hadn't caught them. I was exhausted. I wanted the thing to be done, and I submitted it before I should have. A friend—very kindly— let me know about the errors. And while they weren't mean about it, I was mortified. Not just embarrassed. Ashamed. I felt like I had exposed something broken in myself by putting something out into the world that wasn't polished enough. And if you've spent your whole life trying to avoid being "in trouble," a typo can feel like a character flaw.

That's the thing about shame—it doesn't need to be logical to feel real.

For me, the shame isn't always tied to specific memories. Some of it is broader. A low hum beneath everything. I don't want to disappoint people. I don't want to be called out. I don't want anyone to be mad at me, even if their anger has nothing to do with me. I can feel sick over a misunderstanding that I didn't cause. I can spiral over an unanswered text. I can take a neutral silence and turn it into a full-blown indictment.

It's exhausting.

And it's not the voice of truth. It's the voice of fear.

THE ONLY GOOD THING ABOUT SHAME

The only good thing I've ever discovered about shame is that it keeps us clothed.

That's about it.

Shame isn't guilt. Guilt says, *I did something wrong*. Shame says, *I am something wrong*. And unlike guilt—which can lead to repair—shame just sinks in and settles. It doesn't move us forward. It freezes us in place.

Early in our work together, I asked Debby, the woman who never put herself first from Chapter 4, why she always downplayed her needs—at work, in friendships, even in therapy. She said, "I don't want to be a burden." But when we kept digging, the truth surfaced. She wasn't just afraid of being inconvenient.

She was afraid of being *unlovable* if she ever vocalized her own needs.

She didn't get that message in one loud moment. She absorbed it through years of careful corrections: "Don't be so sensitive." "Be nice." "You're overreacting." "We don't talk about that in this house."

Shame had taught her that expressing emotion meant risking rejection. So she got really good at hiding.

And she wasn't alone.

Shame shows up early. A teacher rolls their eyes when we cry. A parent praises quiet compliance but punishes expression. A pastor calls our queerness "a struggle." And before we know it, we've internalized a belief that who we are is too much—or not enough.

The trouble is, shame doesn't sound like trauma. It sounds like your own voice. By the time we're adults, we think we're just being realistic. Or responsible. Or polite. But underneath? We're still trying to outrun the original wound: *If they really knew me, they wouldn't love me.*

And that's terrifying.

I always cringe a little when people—especially those who aren't particularly religious themselves—talk about wanting to take their kids to church so they can "have good values" or "learn right from wrong." I get it. I'm not anti-church. I've seen faith communities offer belonging and meaning and real growth. But I also know how easy it is for shame to sneak in early, long before kids have the developmental tools to untangle it. Concepts like original sin, substitutionary atonement, and eternal damnation are heavy loads for a five-year-old to carry. Most kids don't hear "you are loved unconditionally." They hear "you are bad by default." They don't internalize nuance. They absorb the headline. And often, the headline is: *You are broken. You are wrong. You are a problem that needs fixing.*

But shame doesn't just come from church. It comes from parents who withhold affection unless we perform. From teachers who humiliate us for mistakes. From coaches who reward self-erasure in the name of "team spirit." From a thousand small moments where we learned that the price of being accepted was being smaller, quieter, better.

And once shame gets in, it's sticky. We stop asking what we need. We stop trusting our feelings. We stop showing up fully—because somewhere deep down, we believe we're a liability.

A Brain That Wouldn't Cooperate

John didn't know he had ADHD.

Not until he was nearly forty.

Not until we sat in my office—frustrated, burned out, confused—and started piecing it together.

He'd been fired from multiple jobs. Not for performance exactly—his work was solid when it got done—but for things like attendance. Deadlines. "Unreliability." Even the jobs he loved eventually fell apart. He'd start strong, build rapport, impress his supervisors. And then he'd miss one too many shifts. Forget one too many details. Let one too many emails go unanswered.

"I swear I'm trying," he said. "I don't know what's wrong with me."

And that's where the shame lived—not in the struggle itself, but in the belief that the struggle meant he was fundamentally flawed.

John was never the "hyper" kid. He didn't bounce off walls or shout in class. He wasn't disruptive—he was funny. Smart. Charming. A little scattered, maybe, but nothing that raised alarms. He got by on last-minute papers and charisma. No one suspected ADHD. No one looked for it. And so no one found it.

But the symptoms were always there—just quieter.

Time blindness.

Mental clutter.

Emotional dysregulation.

A never-ending pile of laundry and unopened mail and shame.

By the time we met, John had internalized every criticism he'd ever received.

Lazy.

Disorganized.

Unreliable.

A mess.

"I thought I just didn't try hard enough. Like I was a screw-up with potential. Someone who could do better if I really wanted to."

That's what undiagnosed ADHD does—it turns executive dysfunction into a character flaw. It masks itself in compliance and cleverness. And then when things inevitably fall apart, it whispers, *See? You're the problem.*

We started small. No checklist. No planner. No podcast. Just this:

"What if the problem isn't you? What if you're just trying to fit into a world that wasn't built for the way your brain works?"

He blinked. Then laughed. Then cried.

"No one's ever said that to me."

Because that's the other thing about neurodivergence—it doesn't just create functional struggles. It creates identity-level shame. You're not just disorganized. You're a disappointment. You're not just forgetful. You're failing. You're not just tired. You're too much.

John had spent years trying to function like a neurotypical person in systems that weren't built for him. He masked. He overcompensated. He faked it. And it almost worked—until it didn't.

That's what we worked on: not just symptom management, but narrative repair. A new story. One where his brain wasn't a liability. Where rest wasn't laziness. Where structure was a support, not a punishment. Where his struggle didn't make him unworthy—it just made him misunderstood.

Sometimes, soul alignment isn't about uncovering some deep trauma. Sometimes, it's about finally naming the thing that's been there all along —and realizing you're not broken.

You're just not built for the rulebook you've been forced to follow.

QUICK CHECK-IN: WHAT'S STILL STICKING?

Shame doesn't always announce itself. Sometimes it sounds like "I should've known better." Or "I don't want to make a big deal out of it." Or "This is probably my fault."

Sometimes it shows up in rituals we don't question anymore—closing our eyes when we pray, apologizing for having a need, re-reading a text five times before we hit send.

So here's a moment to pause:

- *What rule are you still following—even if no one's enforcing it?*
- *What's one area of your life where you fear "getting it wrong"?*
- *What voice in your head sounds like it's protecting you, but might actually be keeping you small?*

You're not broken for feeling this way. You're not behind.

This is what unlearning sounds like. Keep going.

SHAME VOICE

I once worked with a client named Marcus who lived with that same hum of shame. He was in his mid-forties, well-liked at work, good at his job, and constantly anxious that he wasn't doing enough.

Marcus didn't come to therapy in crisis. He came in *polite*. Friendly. Responsible. And deeply unsure of his own worth. "I just always feel like I'm one mistake away from being found out," he said one session, after a long pause. "Like there's something wrong with me and everyone else just hasn't noticed yet."

Marcus grew up in a religious household where obedience was prized and emotions were private. He got good grades. Never got into trouble. Said please and thank you. But any time he spoke up or pushed back, he was met with, *"Don't be difficult,"* or *"That's not very respectful,"* or *"You're just being dramatic."*

He learned quickly that *being easy to be around* was the safest path. And that meant burying anything that felt disruptive—like sadness, or anger, or ambition.

When we started talking about how he managed conflict, he got visibly uncomfortable. "I just try to smooth it over," he said. "I can usually fix it. I just... don't want anyone to think I'm a problem."

It took a while for him to name what he'd been carrying: not guilt for something he'd done, but shame for simply being himself. For having needs. For taking up space.

He told me, "Even when I say something smart in a meeting, I immediately wonder if I sounded arrogant. I'm always editing myself. Even when I'm right."

That's what shame does. It turns you into your own censor.

Shame lives in the nervous system. It makes you flinch before the criticism even comes. It makes you apologize for simply existing. And over time, it erodes your connection to your own voice.

The most important work Marcus did wasn't dramatic. He didn't confront his parents or quit his job or reinvent his life. He just started paying attention to when that inner alarm sounded—and asking whether it actually made sense.

"Most of the time," he told me, "I realize I haven't done anything wrong. I just feel like I have."

That distinction changed everything.

Because when you start naming the shame voice as something *external* —something you inherited, not something you chose—you finally have the option to stop following it.

I've started noticing that same shift in myself.

My shame voice is fast. It's loud. It wants me to explain myself, fix things, get it right. It tries to protect me from humiliation by keeping me in a permanent state of apology.

My real voice is slower. Calmer. Less interested in being right and more interested in being real.

It asks, *Is this actually about you? Are you in trouble, or just afraid? What would it feel like to believe you are already enough?*

RECLAIMING MY NAME

There's one more thing I've never quite known what to do with: my name.

Kirk means "church." My last name is Sheppard. So, you know. Shepherd the Church. Could it be any more on the nose?

I didn't think about it much as a kid. But when I got to Bible college, where most of us were studying to become pastors, it started to feel... loaded. Like there was a cosmic assignment hidden in there that I wasn't fulfilling.

I started as a youth ministry major, but when I realized that job was more about water balloon fights and pies in the face, I bowed out and pursued counseling. (No shade on my friends who did become youth ministers-it just wasn't for me.)

At first, I had shame about this. Since I wasn't named Empathy McFeely, I felt as if I was betraying my destiny.

But now?

Now I see it differently.

I may not be in a pulpit, but I do shepherd a flock. It's not a traditional congregation. It's not bound by a building or a denomination. But in my roles—as a therapist, a writer, a friend—I guide people through dark places. I help them see themselves more clearly. I hold space for truth, and grief, and curiosity. I invite people to return to themselves.

It's not the kind of church I grew up with. But it's sacred all the same.

And maybe that's what alignment looks like: not rejecting who you are, but reclaiming what it means. Taking back the story. Letting your own voice narrate it this time.

QUICK CHECK-IN: SHAME OR SOMETHING ELSE?

Pause for a second and think about the last time you felt uneasy after an interaction.

Now ask yourself:

- *What story did you tell yourself afterward?*
- *Did you assume you did something wrong—even without evidence?*
- *Did you over-apologize, over-explain, or over-edit?*
- *Were you trying to be understood... or just trying not to be misunderstood?*

You're not on trial. You're just noticing. Because once you start naming the voice of shame, you don't have to obey it anymore.

LIGHTNING BUGS AND EARTHWORMS

Nathan was a mid-level manager at a local bank—sharp, organized, articulate, and completely allergic to feedback.

That's not how he described himself, though. When he came to therapy, he framed the problem as everyone else's incompetence. His employees were lazy. His peers were soft. His boss didn't appreciate how hard he worked. And there was always a reason why someone else was to blame.

But underneath that blame was shame—coiled, raw, and ready to strike.

He didn't come in a mess. He came in prepared. Respectful. Efficient. He wore crisp dress shirts and corrected his grammar mid-sentence. He was the kind of client who said things like, "I know I should reframe that," before I could even open my mouth. But when we got close to anything tender—anything that might imply he had something to work on—his posture shifted. His voice tightened. He'd change the subject, usually with a joke or a complaint about someone else's shortcomings.

It wasn't arrogance. It was armor.

Nathan had grown up in a home where excellence was expected but never affirmed. His father—an engineer—demanded perfection, especially from his oldest son. Mistakes weren't corrected, they were punished. Emotion wasn't soothed, it was shamed. And every time Nathan tried to express himself, he was met with a version of, "Don't be soft. Just fix it."

So he fixed it. He became efficient. Polished. Successful. But he also became deeply reactive to any suggestion that he wasn't enough. Because somewhere underneath it all, he still believed it.

And that's the tricky thing about shame. If it's not discharged with honesty, it will leak out as blame.

The work with Nathan was slow. I had to be careful not to push too hard too fast, because shame thrives in urgency. I could see the storm brewing anytime I reflected something back to him that didn't match the story he was telling. He'd nod, then shift the topic. He wasn't ready to look too closely. Not yet.

But session by session, we stayed in the room together. I tried to model what he'd never had: Kindness. Empathy. Patience. Time.

We called it the KEPT approach.

Whenever he felt his irritation rise—at work, with his ex-wife, even with his young son—I encouraged him to pause and remember what we were practicing:

- **Kindness**: What would it look like to respond instead of react?
- **Empathy**: Could he imagine what the other person was feeling?
- **Patience**: Could he give them space to grow at their own pace, not his?

- **Time**: Could he invest in relationship, not just correction?

He wasn't always successful. Sometimes he still defaulted to sarcasm or stormed out of work meetings. But other times, he paused. He softened. He listened. And he started spending more time with his son—not just managing his behavior, but playing, talking, being.

The breakthrough came during a session when Nathan told me about a parenting win.

"I was about to snap," he said. "He was whining, and I could hear my dad's voice in my head, ready to come out of my mouth. And I just... stopped. I sat down beside him. I asked him what was really going on. And he cried. And so did I."

He looked away after telling me that, ashamed again—but this time, of how long it had taken him to get there.

"You broke the cycle," I said. "That's what matters."

He's not perfect. He still gets defensive sometimes. He still wants to be right more than he wants to be real. But he's learning.

And I understood Nathan in a particular way—because I've been him, too.

Years ago, in a supervisor meeting, I remember feeling so frustrated with the pace of conversation. People were saying the most unhelpful, obvious, or downright silly things. I sat there, stewing, trying not to roll my eyes audibly. Heidi, my boss, caught my gaze and gave me a look. It was part reassurance, part validation, and part warning.

Afterward, she pulled me aside.

"Kirk," she said gently, "I know you don't realize it, but you're a lightning bug."

I blinked at her.

"You light up a room. You move fast. You see the connections instantly. But sometimes you're surrounded by earthworms. And it's your job to help light their way."

She didn't shame me. She didn't tell me to dim my light. She showed me that I was seen—and then reminded me of my responsibility.

That's what alignment looks like. Not pretending you're not gifted. Not shrinking to fit in. But learning to offer your light in a way that invites others forward instead of burning them down.

You don't need to dim your light for others—but you do need to recognize how brightly it shines.

SOUL AUDIT: SHAME & STORY

Shame sounds like urgency, apology, and fear. Alignment sounds like your real voice—steady, curious, and kind.

Check all that apply:

- ☐ I assume I'm in trouble when someone says, "Can we talk?"
- ☐ I over-apologize, even when I haven't done anything wrong
- ☐ I've mistaken humility for disappearing
- ☐ **I can tell when the voice in my head is shame—and when it's actually me**
- ☐ **I'm rewriting old beliefs I didn't choose but still carried**
- ☐ **I believe I can live a life that reflects my own truth—not someone else's version**

You don't have to carry shame to be responsible. You don't have to shrink to be good. You don't have to stay small to stay safe.

You get to question the script. You get to speak in your own voice. And you get to decide what kind of story you want to tell next.

FROM THE AUDIT TO ACTION

AWARENESS

Shame isn't always loud. Sometimes it whispers in a voice you mistake for your own. It sounds like correction. Like apology. Like, *"Don't be difficult."* But it's not you—it's a script you absorbed.

Ask yourself:

- *What do I feel guilty about—even when I haven't done anything wrong?*
- *What makes me flinch before I speak, move, or create?*
- *Where do I edit myself for imagined criticism that hasn't even come yet?*
- *Whose voice is that—and is it still welcome in my story?*

Shame thrives in secrecy. But you're allowed to name it, question it, and outgrow it.

PRACTICE

This week, rewrite one line in your internal script.

When you hear the shame voice?

Pause.

Ask: *"Is this mine?"*

Then respond with truth—not performance. Try something like:

"I'm not in trouble. I'm just uncomfortable."

"This isn't a moral failure. It's a typo."

"I get to exist without apologizing."

I wonder . . .what would Kindness, Empathy, Patience, and Time sound like as your own inner voice?

You don't need permission to take the pen back. The story is still unfolding—and your voice gets to lead the next chapter.

CHAPTER 10
THIS MIGHT HURT A LITTLE

I ONCE SPENT my birthday alone at Disney World.

That might sound depressing, but honestly, it wasn't. I love solo trips. I can do what I want, when I want, with no obligation to anyone else. I don't have to wait for someone else to be ready. I don't have to negotiate ride preferences or dining plans. I just go. It's peaceful. It's freeing. (I value *independence*, remember.)

Earlier that morning, the cast member at my hotel had asked if I was celebrating anything special during my stay. When I said it was my birthday, she handed me a little round button and encouraged me to wear it proudly. I hesitated. I wasn't sure I wanted that kind of attention. But I pinned it on anyway.

And something unexpected happened.

All day long—on the bus, in the parks, standing in line, walking through shops—people wished me a happy birthday. Ride operators. Custodians. Other guests. "Happy birthday, Kirk!" they'd say, and smile. Just that. Simple acknowledgment. Just kindness.

It was lovely.

And it caught me off guard how much I liked it.

I'd thought the button would make me feel exposed. What it actually made me feel was seen.

I'd made a dinner reservation that evening at the Plaza Inn, right at the end of Main Street—the perfect place to wrap up the day. When I booked it online, there'd been a little box asking if I was celebrating anything. I'd checked "Birthday," thinking maybe I'd get a free dessert or a little extra sprinkle of Disney magic. Nothing major.

Dinner went smoothly. I sat at my table alone, enjoying the atmosphere, watching families pass by with mouse ears and matching shirts. I felt content. Independent. Grown-up.

And then the server came out of the kitchen holding a cupcake with a lit candle in it.

He walked into the dining room like a showman and announced, "Ladies and gentlemen, there's someone very special with us today!"

I looked around the restaurant, curious who the VIP might be.

And then he kept going.

"The only *problem* is," he said, "he's celebrating his birthday all alone. So we need to sing Happy Birthday to him to make him feel better."

My stomach dropped. My face flushed. There was no question who he was talking about.

The entire restaurant turned to look at me.

I wanted to disappear under the table. But I didn't. I smiled, kind of. I endured the song. And yes—I ate the free cupcake. But the whole thing left me feeling humiliated. Not because I was alone, but because someone had framed my aloneness as a problem to be fixed. He didn't mean harm. I know that. But instead of celebrating me, it felt like I was being pitied. Like I was being put on display.

I had come to Disney alone on purpose. But now I was alone in a spotlight, and it felt awful.

And here's the thing: both moments—the birthday button and the restaurant scene—involved attention. But only one felt good.

That's the difference between vulnerability and violation. One is invited; the other not so much.

And if you've been put on display too many times, you might start avoiding all vulnerability—even the kind that could help you heal.

IF I CAN'T CARRY IT ALL

There's a moment in Disney's *Encanto* that wrecks me every time I see it.

Luisa—the strongest member of the Madrigal family—has spent her whole life carrying both physical and emotional burdens. She's the dependable one, the one everyone turns to, the one who doesn't break. Until she does. And in her big musical number, she sings:

> *"If I could shake the crushing weight of expectations, would that free some room up for joy?*
> *Or relaxation? Or simple pleasure?"*

And then the line that gutted me:

> *"Who am I if I can't carry it all?"*

I've asked that question in my own way more times than I can count. Who am I if I let someone down? If I drop the ball? If I say no, disappoint someone, don't perform, don't show up how they expect me to? Who am I if I can't carry it all?

Those are the questions underneath so much of our burnout and busyness.

Not "Can I handle this?" but "Will I still be loved if I don't?"

Not "What's sustainable?" but "What happens to my worth if I say I'm overwhelmed?"

Luisa's song hit me hard not just because of her strength—but because of her fear.

The fear that if she isn't doing something extraordinary, she's not enough.

That if she can't carry the load, she has no role. No place. No identity.

I've lived in that fear. I bet you have, too. But good news—we don't have to.

THE RISK OF BEING REAL

Vulnerability is one of those words we throw around a lot, but I'm not sure we always know what it means.

It's not confession. It's not oversharing for applause. It's not standing on a stage sobbing into a microphone or writing tell-all essays for clout —or at least, it shouldn't be.

But vulnerability is risk. It's letting yourself be known when the outcome is uncertain. It's telling the truth without being able to control the response.

It's the moment before the feedback comes in. It's hitting "publish." It's walking into a room full of people who don't know you yet—and choosing not to become a curated version of yourself to win them over faster.

Vulnerability is choosing to be seen. On purpose.

And it's terrifying.

I've always had a complicated relationship with being seen. I'm great on stage. I love being the host, the performer, the one with the mic. But that kind of visibility is curated. Controlled. I get to pick the script, the tone, the exits. I'm not just being seen—I'm directing the seeing. That's not vulnerability. That's strategy.

The truth is, I hate when people sing "Happy Birthday" to me at restaurants. I don't like surprise parties. I don't like being caught off guard. I've spent most of my life trying to control the impression I give off, because I believed that was the only way to stay safe.

So yes—I can talk about emotions. I can go deep. I can write whole books about honesty and healing. But sometimes the most intimate thing I can do is let someone see me when I'm not trying at all.

When I'm not polished. Not performing. Just... there.

That's the hardest part. Not telling the story, but letting someone witness the in-between. The unedited version. The version that doesn't have a conclusion yet.

And here's the vulnerable part: I still want to be loved for who I really am—but I also want to make sure I'm seen at my very best while someone is deciding whether they love me or not.

That's the tightrope of vulnerability: wanting to be known while still fearing the cost of being fully open.

But I'm learning. I'm learning that the most meaningful moments in my life haven't come from performance—but from presence. When I wasn't selling a version of myself. When I wasn't rehearsed. When I just showed up, awkward and honest and fully human.

Not dramatic. Not curated.

Just real.

That's the risk. And that's the invitation.

Because the people who love you for your highlight reel aren't the ones who will stay when the lighting changes. But the ones who see you in the quiet moments—who don't flinch at the unpolished version—that's where it starts to feel safe. That's where healing begins.

Not with a spotlight.

But with someone who says, "You don't have to perform here. Just be."

QUICK CHECK-IN

Think about the last time you felt truly seen.

Not praised. Not applauded. Not celebrated for doing something impressive. But known—for who you actually are.

How did it feel? Where were you? Who were you with? What version of yourself showed up?

Now think about the last time you edited yourself to fit in.

- To stay liked.
- To avoid being misunderstood.
- To dodge the discomfort of being seen too clearly.
- What did you hide?
- What did it cost?

You don't have to answer with certainty. Just notice what stirs.

That noticing? That's vulnerability, too.

THE STORY BENEATH THE SMILE

Remember Debby? We've talked about how she gave and gave—meals, energy, emotional labor—but rarely made space for herself. How she stayed in motion to avoid being seen too closely. How her kindness was often camouflage.

But in therapy, something started to shift.

She still greeted me with a smile every week. Still asked how I was, still complimented my shoes, still showed up early and perched on the edge of the couch. But under the warmth, I could feel the weariness. Her body told the truth her words hadn't caught up to yet.

One day, after a long silence, I asked how she was doing.

"Oh, I'm fine," she said, reflexively. And then—something in her eyes changed.

"No, I'm not," she added, barely above a whisper. "I don't think I've been fine for years."

It wasn't dramatic. She didn't cry. She didn't collapse. But that quiet correction was a breakthrough. It was the first time she questioned the script she'd been reciting her whole life.

Debby had learned to be safe by staying small. To be lovable by being useful. To be accepted by staying agreeable. Her helpfulness had become her armor—and connection, the thing she longed for most, felt threatening if it wasn't earned.

"I want to be loved," she told me. "But I also want to stay in control."

That's the paradox of vulnerability. We crave closeness but fear the exposure it requires. And when you're used to being the caregiver, the one who's always fine, it feels radical to admit that you're not.

The work we did wasn't loud or linear. It was slow. Gentle. We practiced asking for help in small ways. Letting silence sit longer. Telling the truth without rushing to soften it.

She stopped bringing snacks to session and started bringing her actual self.

She still wrestles with the urge to disappear—especially when things feel uncertain. But she's learning that her value isn't measured in casseroles or crisis management. It's measured in presence. In honesty. In allowing herself to be seen.

And now, when she says "I'm fine," she pauses. Checks. And sometimes tells the truth instead.

WHAT WE REALLY MEAN BY VULNERABILITY

Let's pause for a second and define something clearly.

Vulnerability isn't a performance. It's not dramatic confession. It's not dumping your story on someone who hasn't earned it. That's exposure —and exposure without trust isn't intimacy. It's risk without relationship. And it can hurt more than it heals.

Vulnerability is something else entirely.

It's choosing to be seen *on purpose.* It's saying, "Actually, I'm not fine," even when your smile is convincing. It's telling the truth without knowing how it will land. It's showing up with your real self—not your rehearsed one—and trusting that who you are is enough, even if you're still figuring it out.

Vulnerability is emotionally honest engagement with someone who has earned access. It's what turns connection into intimacy. It's what allows us to feel known—not just liked, not just admired, but truly seen.

And yes, it's terrifying.

Even when it goes well, it can leave you reeling. That feeling? The "should I have shared that?" spiral? That's what Brené Brown calls a vulnerability hangover. It's normal. It doesn't mean you did something wrong. It just means you were real.

So take a breath. Drink some water. Text someone safe. And then, when you're ready:

Keep showing up anyway.

PRACTICING VULNERABILITY (EVEN WHEN IT'S AWKWARD)

Vulnerability doesn't have to be dramatic. You don't need a stage or a deep confessional moment. Most of the time, practicing vulnerability looks like a small choice in a real moment where you'd usually retreat.

So how do you start?

Try this:

• **Name what you're feeling.** Not just the emotion, but the risk underneath. Am I afraid of rejection? Embarrassment? Disappointment? Do I fear losing control?

• **Check the space.** Have you earned the right to be vulnerable here? Is the person safe? Will they meet your honesty with compassion—or use it as ammunition later?

• **Start small.** Don't crack yourself open all at once. Try a half-truth that's more honest than your usual script. Say, "That's actually hard for me," or "I've been struggling with something," or "I'm not ready to talk about it all yet, but I didn't want to pretend I was fine."

• **Notice what happens.** Does your body tense or soften? Do you want to run? Do you feel relief? That response is data.

• **Pause before explaining.** Most of us rush to tidy up our honesty. "Here's how I'm feeling—but it's fine! I'm fine! It's not a big deal!" Let yourself just... say the thing. And then breathe.

You'll probably feel a little hungover afterward. That's normal. The rush of self-doubt that comes after you share something real is part of the process. You replay what you said. You worry about how it landed. You wonder if you went too far.

But here's the truth: if you've been performing your way through life, vulnerability will always feel like too much at first. Not because it is—but because it's new.

So give yourself credit for every honest moment. Every brave pause. Every time you speak without the mask. Vulnerability isn't weakness. It's strength without armor. And strength like that takes practice.

You don't have to get it perfect. You just have to keep trying.

I don't think vulnerability ever stops being scary. But I do think it gets easier to recognize when it's worth the risk. It's in the quiet ask for help. The "I'm not okay" text to a friend. The email you reread ten times before hitting send. It's in the moment you stop talking and finally listen to what your body's been trying to say.

And maybe—if I'm lucky—the next time someone hands me a cupcake with a candle in it, I won't panic. I'll just let it be a moment of kindness I didn't have to earn.

SOUL AUDIT: VULNERABILITY & VISIBILITY

Vulnerability isn't about overexposure. It's about showing up without pretending—and trusting that your softness isn't a liability.

Check all that apply:

- ☐ I present a polished version of myself to avoid being misunderstood
- ☐ I've stayed silent to avoid looking weak or needy
- ☐ I long for connection, but try to control how I'm seen
- ☐ **I can name at least one person who sees me without performance**
- ☐ **I've taken a risk by being real, even when I felt exposed**
- ☐ **I'm learning that vulnerability doesn't mean reckless —it means honest**

Vulnerability doesn't require you to tell everyone everything. You don't have to rip your heart open on command.

But you do deserve spaces where you can show up as you are—unpolished, unguarded, and still welcomed.

That's not exposure. That's visibility.

That's not recklessness. That's trust.

And that's where real connection begins.

FROM THE AUDIT TO ACTION

AWARENESS

You don't have to perform to be worthy.

You don't have to impress to be included.

And you don't have to wait until it's polished or perfect to let yourself be seen.

Ask yourself:

- *Where am I still offering a curated version of myself?*
- *What part of me have I been keeping quiet—not out of wisdom, but out of fear?*
- *Who are my safe people—and when's the last time I let them see the real me?*
- *Where am I bracing for rejection, even when no one's actually walking away?*

You're allowed to show up before you're certain. Before you're fine. Before it's ready.

PRACTICE

Choose one small act of realness this week. Not for shock. Not for applause. Just for truth.

- *Send a text that says, "I miss you."*
- *Share a feeling before you're sure how it'll land.*
- *Wear something that makes you feel like you.*
- *Let someone see your face soften. Or your guard lower. Or your eyes well up.*

You don't have to explain why you're alone with a birthday cupcake in the most magical place on Earth.

You just have to believe you deserve the song.

CHAPTER 11
SOMETHING WORTH LETTING GO

I WAS TAUGHT that it was **unforgivable** not to forgive others.

That sentence sounds dramatic, but it was presented as spiritual fact. You had to forgive. Period. That was the deal: God it for us, so He expected that we do it, too. And if you didn't? Then you were the problem. Not the person who hurt you. Not the situation that broke your heart. If you couldn't forgive, the failure was *yours*.

It feels like a setup. A neat little theological trap for people already weighed down with shame.

For a long time, I thought forgiving quickly made me mature, holy, generous. But real forgiveness isn't a moral performance; it's a personal release. It's not about making the other person feel better. That's mercy. That's a gift you give someone else. Forgiveness, real forgiveness, is something you do for yourself.

Forgiveness isn't about the other person at all. It's about letting go of the bitterness that slowly erodes you from the inside out. It's about stopping the cycle of pain replaying in your head, the clenched jaw when their name comes up, the quiet urge to keep rehearsing the argument you'll never get to finish.

Forgiveness isn't forgetting. It's not reconciliation. It's not approval. And it is absolutely not the absence of boundaries. You cannot forgive someone who is actively, currently hurting you in the exact same way they always have. You can't forgive what hasn't stopped. That's not forgiveness—it's surrender. And it isn't noble. It isn't grace. It's self-erasure dressed up as virtue.

QUICK CHECK-IN

Before we go any further, I want to ask you something.

- *Have you ever said, "I forgive you," but felt it catch in your throat?*
- *Have you ever let something go because you thought you were supposed to—only to find that your body still braced every time their name came up?*
- *Have you ever wondered if maybe... just maybe... what you called forgiveness was actually just submission?*

If so, you're not alone.

What comes next isn't about judgment. It's about curiosity. It's about noticing when your version of "forgiveness" was really just a quieter way of disappearing.

It's about reclaiming what forgiveness actually means.

LOVE SHOULDN'T HURT LIKE THIS

Nicole had worked her whole life to create stability. She had money. A high-level white-collar job. A reputation for excellence. She was driven, reliable, respected. The kind of person who managed everything on the outside, even when everything on the inside was unraveling.

She also had a deep, unrelenting ache to be loved. And when she met Steve—at a bar, of all places—she thought maybe this was it. He was charming in a rough-edged way. Quick with affection. Intense with praise. He told her she was beautiful. Told her he'd never met anyone like her.

The relationship moved fast. There were red flags, sure. But she wanted to believe that this was true love.

So when she found out he used meth, she was concerned—but forgiving. He said he was getting clean. That he'd only relapsed because of stress. That he just needed stability. Someone who believed in him. Someone like her.

And when he disappeared for days at a time and came back blaming her —saying she was too controlling, that he needed space, that she didn't understand—she still welcomed him in. Because she didn't want to be harsh. Because she didn't want to give up on someone she loved. Because she believed forgiveness was a virtue.

But slowly, bit by bit, Nicole was losing everything she'd worked for.

Her savings dwindled. Her emotional bandwidth disappeared. Her friendships grew distant because she was tired of making excuses. She was unraveling—and still, she told herself that what she was doing was good. That she was being faithful. That she was forgiving.

But what she was really doing... was enabling.

She wasn't forgiving from a place of power. She was surrendering from a place of shame.

The tricky thing about shame-based identities is that they're really good at looking virtuous. Nicole believed that staying with Steve was a sign of strength. She thought her willingness to forgive made her loyal, kind, generous. She framed it as grace, even love. In her mind, she was proving something—to Steve, to herself, maybe even to God. But underneath all of that virtue was a belief she couldn't quite name: that she didn't actually deserve anything better. Somewhere along the way, she'd been taught that real love meant endurance. That pain was part of the deal.

That to be chosen, you had to be willing to suffer. So she stayed. She "forgave." Over and over.

But the truth is, real love doesn't require pain as proof. And real forgiveness doesn't require you to bleed.

I told Nicole what I'll tell you: you don't owe anyone your destruction in the name of redemption. You don't have to stay in harm's way to prove that you have character. You don't need to collapse just to be considered compassionate. Forgiveness, when it's real, belongs to you. It's not something you're obligated to offer on someone else's timeline. You get to define it. You get to decide when you're ready. And most importantly, you get to draw the line between letting go—and letting back in.

What Forgiveness Actually Looks Like

Forgiveness isn't a one-time event. It's a process. And like any process, it's allowed to be messy, non-linear, and entirely on your terms.

Here's what I offer clients who are working through it—not as a prescription, but as a map with more than one road:

- **Step One: Name what happened.**
  - Not the softened version. Not the version that makes them look better or makes you look worse. The truth.
- **Step Two: Feel what you feel.**
  - Anger. Sadness. Betrayal. Rage. All of it belongs. You can't move through what you refuse to acknowledge.
- **Step Three: Decide what you want to let go of—and what you still need.**
  - Maybe you're ready to release the constant replay in your head. Maybe you're not ready to release the anger yet. That's okay. Forgiveness doesn't require erasing. It requires clarity.

- **Step Four: Set a boundary, if you need one.**
  - Forgiveness doesn't have to mean reconciliation. You can let go and still say, "And I'm not letting you back in."
- **Step Five: Choose your moment.**
  - If and when forgiveness comes, let it be real. Let it feel like ease. Like something in your body relaxes, even just a little.

You don't have to forgive loudly. You don't even have to tell the other person. Sometimes, forgiveness is a quiet decision you make alone, in your own time, with no audience.

And if you're not there yet? That's not a failure. That's part of the work.

SOUL AUDIT: FORGIVENESS & ALIGNMENT

Forgiveness isn't about being good—it's about being honest. It's not a spiritual shortcut. It's a reckoning with what's true.

Check all that apply:

- ☐ I've offered forgiveness out of obligation—not readiness
- ☐ I've confused forgiveness with reconciliation or approval
- ☐ I've stayed in harm's way because I thought leaving meant failing
- **☐ I know now that healing doesn't require access to the person who caused the harm**
- **☐ I've started forgiving myself—not just for what I did, but for how long I carried it**
- **☐ I can name at least one resentment I'm ready to set down—even if just a little**

You don't have to rush to forgive. You don't have to forget to move forward.

Forgiveness begins when you tell the truth—about what hurt, what it cost, and what you're no longer willing to carry.

It's not performance. It's release. And it belongs to you.

FROM THE AUDIT TO ACTION

AWARENESS

Forgiveness isn't a shortcut to virtue. It's not a bypass around pain. And it's not a performance for the sake of being seen as good. Real forgiveness begins with truth—not obligation.

Ask yourself:

- *Where am I offering forgiveness before I've even felt the hurt?*
- *Have I confused letting go with letting someone back in?*
- *What version of "being good" still asks me to disappear in order to forgive?*
- *Where might forgiveness serve me—not them?*

You don't have to hand out grace on someone else's timeline. You get to heal first.

PRACTICE

This week, try one of these:

- *Write a letter you never send. Name what happened. Name what it cost.*
- *Say (even just to yourself), "I'm not ready to forgive that yet."*
- *Ask: "Is my forgiveness coming from freedom—or fear?"*
- *Practice forgiveness in the hardest place: toward yourself.*

Real forgiveness doesn't silence your truth. It honors it. And when you're ready, it helps you lay it down—not because you should, but because you're free to.

CHAPTER 12
NOTHING'S MISSING
EXCEPT WHAT'S GONE

I THINK ABOUT THE "WHAT IFS" a lot.

What if my dad hadn't died when I was six?

What if I'd had more access to the arts when I was young—or just the guts to try creative things sooner?

What if I'd gone to a secular university instead of Bible college?

What if I'd played football in high school? What would life have been like had I joined a frat? Married a woman? Had kids?

What if I'd come out earlier?

While these questions are just hypothetical now, they're rooted in missed opportunities or paths I didn't take. They likely would have led to versions of myself I never got to be.

The pain that comes with this is grief. Not the loud, sobbing kind. The quiet kind. The kind that sneaks in when you're driving or brushing your teeth or scrolling Instagram and wondering how someone else ended up with a life that feels like it *could've* been yours.

What I realize, though, is that while I don't believe in destiny or fate, I do think that my life turned out the way it was supposed to. No matter which paths I could have taken or the universe could have chosen for me, I'd still be doing what I do now.

I'm not necessarily living the life I imagined. But I'm living the one I *chose*. And that matters.

So yeah—I still grieve the "what ifs." But I don't live there anymore. I've got a life now. And I like it. But some people don't get to that point right away. Some people don't get to choose the life they're handed—not until it cracks open.

NOT JUST THE INJURY

Grief is often painted as something clean. A loss, a goodbye, a funeral. But most of the grief I see doesn't come with that kind of clarity. It doesn't arrive all at once. It leaks. It lingers. It hides behind frustration, behind fatigue, behind phrases like "I'm fine" or "It's just been a hard week." The truth is, most grief lives in the unfinished chapters. In the "what could've been." In the moments that feel empty and heavy at the same time.

You've met Ruthie before. When she first came to therapy, it was because of an accident. She'd injured her hand badly. She was trying to adjust to the reality that she wouldn't regain full function. She was angry, understandably, and scared. She hated how the injury slowed her down. How it changed the way people looked at her. She felt like her body had betrayed her, and she didn't want to talk about it. Or at least, she said she didn't.

But she kept showing up.

Every week, she'd come in and sit stiffly across from me, arms folded. Some days, we barely made progress. But other days, she'd crack open just a little. A sentence. A memory. A question. Slowly, something deeper started to emerge. The grief she was carrying wasn't just about her hand—it was about what the hand had represented. Power. Control. Capability. Protection.

And when that was taken, something old and buried started to rise.

Ruthie didn't name it right away. It came out sideways—through defensiveness, anger, and eventually tears. But over time, she started to share pieces of something much heavier than an injury. She talked about growing up afraid. About not being believed. About feeling unprotected. And eventually, the truth surfaced: Ruthie had been sexually abused. She had carried it silently for decades. She had tried to move on, to build a life, to be strong. And in many ways, she had. But the injury to her hand cracked open the part of her that had never really healed.

She was grieving so many things. The fingers she'd lost. The body that no longer felt like hers. The mother who hadn't protected her. The version of herself she'd had to become just to survive.

She thought she came for the injury. But it unearthed something older —something she could no longer ignore.

That's the thing about grief: it doesn't always announce itself. Sometimes it waits for the right opening. A crisis. A crack. An unexpected loss that unlocks all the others. And if you're willing—or brave enough, or tired enough—you let it come.

And then the real healing can begin.

LEAVING INTO ALIGNMENT

I also used to think grief only came with endings. Death. Breakups. Big, dramatic shifts. But I've learned that grief can come with growth, too. Not because something terrible happened, but because something important ended.

Sometimes, we're the one who has to end it.

I left my first counseling job after being offered a raise. A one-cent raise. And to be clear, that wasn't a merit-based increase. I was being paid less than the minimum of the pay band for my position, and so they adjusted my pay to the absolute bottom of the scale—because per policy —they had to. Instead of being given a merit increase for my hard work, my wage was corrected on paper and I was dismissed in spirit. And without saying it, this showed me that I wasn't valued in a way that aligned with my self-assessment . . .or my formal year-end review.

That moment was insulting, yes. But more than that, it was illuminating. I realized they couldn't see who I had become. I'd grown, developed, contributed—but they still saw me as just another employee. Another entry in a spreadsheet full of salaries and pay bands.

There was grief in leaving. Not because I wanted to stay—but because something that had shaped me no longer fit. It had been formative. But I'd outgrown it.

That same ache showed up again when I worked in the emergency department at a children's hospital. While I was one of only two people from our department ever nominated for a prestigious internal award, my boss did not acknowledge it.

She never said congratulations. Never sent an email to the team celebrating me. Never acknowledged the honor at all other than showing up at the obligatory breakfast where she proceeded to chat with a colleague of hers through all of the presentations.

But that wasn't the only time she treated me poorly. When I asked about applying for a promotion, I was told I was too new to the job— even with fifteen years of prior experience in the field. When I submitted my application for clinical advancement, the whole packet was denied because one physical copy—one of many—was missing a single page. I muttered, 'Good thing it wasn't an administrative assistant advancement application,' trying to mask my frustration with a joke.

But it wasn't just the bureaucracy that wore me down. It was the values. I cared about the collaboration with the ED team. About making sure patients were seen and treated safely. My boss wanted something different. She wanted us to spend hours with one kid—never mind the fact that doing so blocked a much-needed emergency room bed, or sent that child home to an unsafe situation just to avoid a psychiatric placement. I couldn't be complicit in that. So I left.

And still—I grieved it.

Because despite the frustration, I loved that job. I loved the staff. I loved being in the middle of the action. And I especially loved the doctors and nurses. When I left, a group of them even took me out to dinner— something that had never happened before when someone from my ancillary team moved on. And yes, I'm bragging. But it matters. It was real connection. Real respect.

I didn't leave because I hated it. I left because I couldn't stay and keep growing.

That's the grief of becoming. It's not always about what you lose. Sometimes it's about what you *can't keep* if you want to stay aligned. Even if it's something good. Even if it still means something to you.

But what I've learned is this: you can miss something and still know you were right to leave. You can carry gratitude and grief at the same time. You can look back with love *and* move forward without regret.

And yes—I still say it, even now, even in therapy sessions:

 "In the words of the great philosopher Elsa the Ice Queen aka Her Majesty Idina Menzel... sometimes we just need to *let it go*."

It sounds silly. But it's true.

Letting go isn't cold. It's not apathy. It's not detachment. Letting go is *alignment in action*. It's what happens when you stop justifying the version of yourself you've outgrown.

To everything there is a season. Some things you hold onto. Some things you release. And when the season shifts, the most aligned thing you can do is recognize it—and move on.

RUBBERY CHICKEN AND THE GRIEF OF ROUTINE

Not all grief comes from loss with a capital L. Sometimes, it shows up in the little routines that quietly stop working.

I'm someone who eats at the same restaurants over and over. Not just because I'm a creature of habit, but because I build relationships. I get to know the staff. I like being recognized. I like having "a place." For a long time, that place was Wings & Rings. I ate there at least twice a week. The boneless wings were great. The vibe was consistent. I knew the people. It was a comfort—one of those steady, easy things that just worked.

Until they changed the wings.

Suddenly, my go-to meal turned into rubbery, frozen pseudo-chicken. I tried to pivot. Switched to chicken tenders. That worked for a while—until they got rid of those too. And just like that, the ritual was gone. I didn't throw a fit or write a Google review. (Well... I might have emailed corporate. And I might have posted on Yelp.) But the point is, I also didn't go back. And I haven't been there in well over a year.

It sounds silly, but I genuinely felt sad about it. I missed the familiarity. The rhythm. The staff I used to chat with. It wasn't about wings—it was about belonging. And it was gone.

Sometimes the grief of becoming is wrapped in things like that. A meal. A place. A version of yourself that no longer fits into your own routines. You try to recreate the comfort, but it doesn't land. And you can't force it. You just have to let it go.

And yes—I hear Elsa in my head again. *Let it go.*

It's not always a dramatic decision. Sometimes it's just noticing that something doesn't feel like home anymore, and choosing to stop pretending that it does.

And then—because life is funny—I found out that the location near my office still has the old boneless wings. And the tenders. And great service. It was like a resurrection. The comfort came back, just in a different location.

It didn't erase the grief of losing the old spot. But it reminded me that letting go doesn't mean you'll never feel at home again. Sometimes you just have to give yourself permission to look somewhere new.

QUICK CHECK-IN: WHAT DOESN'T FIT ANYMORE?

Letting go doesn't always feel dramatic. Sometimes it just feels... off.

So take a breath, and ask yourself:

- *What's something small I've been holding onto—even though it no longer feels like me?*
- *Where have I been showing up out of habit, not alignment?*
- *What old comfort am I still chasing, hoping it'll feel the way it used to?*
- *And what might be waiting for me, if I gave myself permission to look somewhere new?*

Grief isn't always about endings. Sometimes, it's about evolution.

You're not failing if it doesn't fit anymore.

You're just becoming someone else. Someone more aligned.

Let that be okay.

STILL TETHERED, JUST DIFFERENT

Of course, not all grief is about chicken wings. Some grief breaks you in ways no Yelp review can touch. The grief of a changed routine is one thing. But then there's the kind that takes someone from you. The kind that takes your breath with it.

It doesn't just hurt—it disorients. The kind of loss where your brain knows what happened, but your body keeps looking for them. You reach for the phone. You glance toward the chair. You start a text you'll never send. And then you remember. And it hits you all over again.

When it's someone you loved—really loved—someone who knew you on a soul level, someone you didn't have to explain yourself to, someone who laughed at your shorthand jokes and cried when you cried—it doesn't matter how long it's been. Their absence isn't something you get over. It becomes something you live inside of.

When people say, "You'll move on," they don't know. You don't move on from your person. You just slowly learn how to live in a world where they aren't anymore.

Some people lose a spouse. Some lose a parent. Some lose the friend who knew their whole history—the person who showed up when nobody else did. Whoever it is, when they're gone, alignment doesn't feel like a practice. It feels like a betrayal. You don't want to feel better. You want them back.

And sometimes the people around you don't know what to do with your grief. They want it to be tidy. Manageable. They want to know how you're doing in a way that makes *them* feel better. They ask, "Are you okay?" and you say "I'm fine," because the real answer is too complicated, too sacred, too exhausting to explain.

You wonder who you are now that they're not here to see you.

You realize they were the one who remembered your milestones. Who called you out when you were lying to yourself. Who reminded you that you were worthy on the days you forgot. Now that they're gone, there's no one on the other end of that string. You're still tethered—but only to memory.

And yet—somehow—you keep going.

Not because you're strong. Not because you're over it. But because you're becoming someone who knows how to carry it. You're learning how to tell the truth and still get out of bed. How to miss them without losing yourself. How to honor them by living the kind of life they would've wanted for you—not as a performance, but as a quiet act of love.

Soul alignment after deep grief doesn't mean moving forward with joy. It means moving forward with honesty. It means walking with your limp. It means keeping a space in your heart for the love that shaped you, and trusting that nothing—not even death—can take that away.

Letting go doesn't mean forgetting. It doesn't mean you're okay. It simply means you've stopped fighting the fact that they're gone. And in that surrender, something sacred opens. Not closure.

But maybe—a kind of peace.

And if you're in that place—missing someone who anchored you—here are a few ways to carry the grief with care:

- **Honor the memory. Don't try to forget.**
  - Set a place at the dinner table on their birthday. Watch their favorite movie. Tell their stories. You're not stuck in the past—you're in relationship with it.
- **Let yourself get angry.**
  - Be mad they left. Be mad at the unfairness. Anger doesn't cancel the love—it gives it shape. It's part of how you reckon with the loss.
- **Say what you didn't get to say.**
  - Write the letter. Speak it out loud. Light a candle. The conversation doesn't have to end. You can still say what's true.
- **Let joy visit—even if it feels like a betrayal.**

- ○ Laugh. Dance. Go to their favorite diner and order their usual. You don't have to choose between grief and aliveness. You get to have both.

SOUL AUDIT: GRIEF

Grief doesn't always look like mourning. Sometimes it looks like fatigue. Or frustration. Or the quiet ache of what might've been.

Alignment begins when we name what's missing—and what we've become in its absence.

Check all that apply:

- ☐ I've grieved something quietly because it didn't "seem big enough"
- ☐ I miss a version of myself I had to leave behind to keep growing
- ☐ I still flinch when I remember how something ended—even if it was the right choice
- **☐ I've let myself feel something all the way through— even when it surprised me**
- **☐ I can name at least one thing I've released that made room for something new**
- **☐ I'm learning that grief and gratitude can live in the same story**

There's no right pace for grieving. If something caught in your throat while reading this, take note. You're not stuck. You're just still becoming. **And grief might be part of the way forward.**

FROM THE AUDIT TO ACTION

AWARENESS

Grief isn't a flaw in your process. It's part of becoming. And becoming something new always means leaving something behind—sometimes with gratitude, sometimes with heartbreak, often with both.

Ask yourself:

- *Where in my life have I changed, but haven't yet mourned the change?*
- *What loss am I still holding onto—not because I need to, but because I'm afraid to release it?*
- *Where am I calling it "burnout" when it's really grief?*
- *What goodbye have I outlived—but not yet acknowledged?*

There is no timeline for loss. But there *is* permission to name it.

PRACTICE

If you're ready:

- *Write a short letter to something you've lost—someone, somewhere, or some version of yourself.*
- *Don't edit it. Don't spiritualize it. Just speak plainly: what you miss, what it meant, what you're ready to release.*

Then say this, out loud if you can:

"I don't have to carry this alone anymore. I'm still me. And I'm still becoming."

Letting go doesn't erase your love. It honors it.

CHAPTER 13
STILL FROM THERE, JUST NOT LIKE THAT

SMALL-TOWN LIVING, while charming in Hallmark movies and Frank Capra films, just isn't for me. I especially disliked living on a farm. The dirt, the smells—and the hard work—were not my jam. While I absolutely appreciate farmers and laborers (especially because I don't want to do what they do), I still remember what my grandfather used to say about work: *Work smarter, not harder.* That's probably why I ended up with three degrees and a job where I don't sweat or lift anything heavy.

I grew up in Richwood, Ohio. It's the kind of town where everyone knows everyone—or at least knows *of* everyone. There were about ninety kids in my high school class. We all shopped for groceries at the Richwood Cardinal. People gathered at The Heritage restaurant for coffee and gossip. And nearly everyone was affiliated with a church. Maybe they didn't go every week, but come Easter or Christmas Eve, they had a pew with their name on it.

But even in a place that familiar, I didn't feel known. Not really. I grew up with secrets, and when you carry secrets, you learn to perform. I was homecoming king, student council president, editor of both the newspaper and the yearbook. On paper, I had it all together. But no one knew my fears, my desires, my worries, or my struggles. I'm not sure I knew them either.

When people ask where I'm from, I still hesitate. If it's someone local to Cincinnati, I'll say Richwood—a small farm town about an hour north-west of Columbus. Marion, Marysville, and Delaware are the bigger towns nearby that people have probably heard of. It's important to distinguish that I'm an immigrant, because native to Cincinnati ask "what high school did you go to?"

Trust me, it's a thing.

But if the person asking isn't from here, I'll usually just say Cincinnati. I've lived here since 1996, when I came for college and never really left. Sometimes I'll even say Dayton, Kentucky—where I live now—but that gets confusing thanks to Dayton, Ohio.

My answer depends on who's asking and what I think they really want to know. And that's the heart of cultural identity—not just where you're from, but which parts of yourself you've learned to reveal or withhold depending on the room you're in.

It's not just geography. It's knowing what version of you feels safe—or acceptable—depending on the context.

Cultural identity is built on traditions, beliefs, language, and rituals—but it's felt most in the quiet of belonging. What part of me fits here? What part doesn't? And what happens when I stop trying to force it?

BEER TENTS AND BINGO

I used to think I didn't really have a culture. I was just "normal." White. From a small town. Church on Sundays. Cornfields and casseroles. But the older I got—and the more rooms I entered where that wasn't the default—the more I realized how much my early environment shaped what I believed was right, safe, or acceptable. And how much I'd have to unlearn to really become myself.

For me, that early environment was the Church of Christ. Not fire and brimstone. Not prosperity gospel. Something quieter. More orderly. You didn't raise your hands during worship. You didn't say "Amen" out loud unless you were the one offering the prayer (with your eyes closed, of course). The roles were clearly defined. Women didn't lead – in public anyway.

Everyone knew the rules, even if they weren't written down. And you didn't just follow them because someone said so. You followed them because they were *everywhere.* In the pews. In the potlucks. In the way people shook your hand at the door.

There was a kind of politeness to it all. A kind of Midwestern restraint that looked like warmth, but often felt like pressure. We were friendly, sure. But it was the kind of friendliness that depended on conformity. If you fit the mold, you were celebrated. If you didn't, you learned quickly how to adjust.

I don't remember ever being explicitly told that emotions were dangerous or inconvenient. But I definitely learned how to keep mine in check. Vulnerability made people uncomfortable. Questioning things made people uncomfortable. Taking up too much space—emotionally or otherwise—was discouraged. We didn't call it shame. We called it humility. We didn't call it avoidance. We called it grace. We didn't call it silence. We called it maturity.

And it was all part of the *culture.*

I grew up very white. And I don't just mean in terms of race—I mean in the sense of cultural conditioning. I learned that success looked like stability, order, good grades, good manners, and a certain kind of quiet pride. I learned that "helping others" often meant being seen as generous or good—but not necessarily being changed by the people you helped. I learned that discomfort was something to be avoided, not explored.

So when I moved to Cincinnati, I didn't think I had much to unlearn. Culturally, the city has a lot of Catholic roots, and some of the rhythms were familiar. People here love a church event. They love a fish fry. They love community. That part made sense to me.

But I'll never forget the moment I found out the church festivals here had beer tents. And Bingo. I was stunned. You drink and gamble at the church?! It felt like heresy to my small-town Protestant bones. I wasn't offended—I was just genuinely baffled. I didn't know you could do that and still be considered holy. And that's when I started to realize how much of my spirituality had been built on *cultural norms*, not personal conviction.

BIG CITIES, BLUNT QUESTIONS

The first time I visited New York City, I realized just how much of my small-town politeness was culturally learned—and how poorly it translated outside the Midwest.

I wasn't afraid of the big buildings or the crowds. I wasn't even rattled by the impatient taxi cabs that brushed my calves at intersections. What shook me was the bus ride from the airport.

I sat in the front seat. Big mistake.

The driver was furious at the world—honking, flipping off other cars, shouting audibly at drivers who couldn't hear him. It felt reckless and personal, like I was one wrong lane change away from death. I kept glancing nervously around the bus, expecting someone else to react—but nobody did. They were calm. Bored, even.

To them, it was Tuesday.

That was my first real clue: New York wasn't dangerous—just different. It was just fast. Direct. Unapologetic. If you needed help, people would gladly point you the right way—but you had to ask quickly. Without a two-minute Midwest warm-up. Without five sentences of throat-clearing politeness. They wouldn't wait around for you to work up to it.

It wasn't that New Yorkers were unfriendly. They just operated by different cultural rules—ones I hadn't been taught.

And in a weird way, that realization made me feel less small.

Because if something as simple as how you asked for directions could change from one place to another, then maybe—just maybe—there were more ways to belong than the one I grew up with.

LEARNING A NEW LANGUAGE

At my first counseling job in Indiana, things still felt familiar. The clients looked like me. Sounded like me. Came from the same kinds of towns I had. I could speak their language without thinking about it. But when I took a new job in a more urban part of Cincinnati, everything shifted. My clients didn't look like me. They didn't talk like me. Their stories were unfamiliar. Their needs felt bigger than my training. And at first, I was scared. I wasn't sure I'd know how to help. I wasn't sure I'd be trusted. I wasn't sure I wouldn't mess it up.

But I stayed. I listened. I asked questions. I read. I unlearned. I leaned into the awkwardness of not knowing. I paid attention to what made me uncomfortable and sat with it instead of trying to fix it.

And slowly, the gap closed.

I stopped seeing my clients through a lens of pity. I stopped seeing them as people to rescue. I started seeing them as resourceful, resilient, brilliant. I started seeing the systems they were navigating. The strength it took to survive. The creativity. The love. I wasn't there to save them. I was there to learn from them. To walk beside them.

That shift didn't just make me a better therapist. It made me more curious. More honest. Less certain. I wasn't trying to serve two cultural worlds anymore or play translator between what I believed and what I felt. I was starting to build something new. Something that honored where I came from, but wasn't bound to it. Something that felt like *mine*. Something aligned.

Cultural identity isn't always about ethnicity or geography. Sometimes it's shaped by your profession, your disability status, your gender expression, or the unwritten rules of your family system. For some people, the culture they're navigating is academic, queer, neurodiverse, military, artistic, or rooted in addiction recovery. Culture can be anything that teaches you how to behave, how to belong, and who you need to be in order to stay safe.

QUICK CHECK-IN

Before we move on, take a breath.

- *What parts of your upbringing shaped the way you see yourself today?*
- *What behaviors were praised? What questions were discouraged?*
- *What assumptions did you inherit about what success, kindness, or faith should look like?*

Cultural identity isn't just about where you're from—it's about what you've absorbed. And if you've never stopped to examine it, you might still be living out a script you didn't choose.

So here's your invitation: pause, notice, and get curious. You don't have to reject your roots to replant yourself.

A MOLD OF HER OWN

Jenny didn't come into therapy to talk about culture. She came in because she was tired—tired of second-guessing herself at work, tired of decoding people's microaggressions in real time, tired of being told she was "so well-spoken," as if it were somehow a surprise. More than anything, she was tired of not feeling at home in her own life.

Her first name was familiar—Jenny. The kind of name that doesn't raise eyebrows on a class roster. But her last name often prompted questions, the kind people ask when they're trying to place you, define you, categorize you. "Where are you from?" they'd ask—not in the casual, hometown sense, but in the coded, "Why do you look like that?" sense. And when she told them she was born and raised in the U.S.—in suburban Cleveland, no less—they'd press further. "No, but where are you *really* from?"

She told me once, with a dry laugh and a soft sort of defiance, "I like horror movies and iced coffee. I've never once called my mom anything but 'Mom.' But people keep trying to assign me a background that makes *them* feel better about *my* identity."

At home, the pressure felt different. Her parents had immigrated from Pakistan before she was born and carried with them not just a language and a legacy, but a deep reverence for the sacrifices they'd made. They worked hard to preserve the culture they left behind, and while Jenny understood Urdu well enough to catch every critique, she wasn't fluent. In their eyes, she was often too American. At school, she had been considered quiet and polite. At work, she was seen as efficient but often overlooked. In every context, she was being read through someone else's lens.

She wasn't confused about who she was. In fact, she liked who she was. Her humor was quick and dry. She knew how to speak with clarity and power when she was in the right space. She wasn't trying to reject her heritage—or over-identify with it. She just wanted to exist without having to constantly justify the way she showed up in the world.

"Sometimes," she told me, "it feels like I'm being asked to prove I belong before I'm allowed to just *be*."

Jenny wasn't looking for belonging in the traditional sense anymore. She wasn't trying to find a new group to fit into, or a new set of values to inherit. What she wanted—what so many people want—was the space to stop contorting herself into a shape that made other people more comfortable. She didn't need to be more of one thing and less of another. She didn't need to "own her heritage" or "embrace her roots" if that didn't feel authentic. She just needed permission to be fully herself —no explanations, no performance.

At some point during our work together, I said, "Maybe you don't need to find the right mold. Maybe you get to make your own."

She didn't respond right away, but she let out a long exhale. It was the kind of breath that signals release. Relief. Recognition. For the first time, someone had suggested she didn't have to choose between parts of herself. She could be both. She could be neither. She could just be Jenny.

That's what cultural alignment looks like. Not assimilation. Not rebellion. But the freedom to stop performing—and the space to belong to yourself.

FROM HERE, BUT CHANGED

I'm still from Richwood. I still believe in front porches, neighborly check-ins, and the comfort of calling someone by their first name like we're related—because we likely are.

I still carry some of the values I was taught growing up—hard work, hospitality, decency—but now I carry them with better language. With less fear. With more clarity. I no longer confuse silence with respect, or shame with maturity, or belonging with sameness.

I'm not pretending I'm not from there. I'm just not pretending I fit there anymore. I don't need to erase where I came from to be who I am now. But I also don't need to shrink back into the mold that raised me. That mold did its job—it held me for a while. But I outgrew it. And that's not betrayal. That's growth.

Cultural alignment isn't about rejecting your roots. And it's not about romanticizing them either. It's about being honest—about what shaped you, about what stayed with you, and about what no longer fits. It's knowing that where you're from is part of your story—but it's not your whole story. You get to decide which parts to carry forward, and which ones you've earned the right to leave behind.

I'm still from there. Just not like that.

SOUL AUDIT: CULTURAL ALIGNMENT

You don't have to reject your roots to honor your truth. Alignment means belonging to yourself—even if you no longer belong in the place you came from.

Check all that apply:

- ☐ I've felt like I had to choose between authenticity and acceptance
- ☐ I've outgrown parts of my identity but still feel guilty for changing
- ☐ I adapt how I show up depending on who I'm with
- ☐ **I can name at least one place or community where I feel fully myself**
- ☐ **I'm starting to redefine what "home" means to me**
- ☐ **I believe I can honor where I'm from without limiting who I'm becoming**

Cultural alignment isn't about erasing your past. It's about choosing what still fits—and releasing what doesn't. Where you started shaped you. But who you're becoming? That's yours to define.

FROM THE AUDIT TO ACTION

AWARENESS

You don't have to rewrite your entire story to live in alignment—but you do have to be honest about what no longer fits.

Cultural identity isn't just about where you're from—it's about what you've internalized to stay safe, stay likable, or stay small.

Ask yourself:

- *What traditions or expectations shaped me—but don't reflect me anymore?*
- *Where do I shrink, code-switch, or self-edit to keep others comfortable?*
- *What beliefs about identity, expression, or belonging did I inherit—but never question?*
- *What would it look like to be more fully myself—even if I don't fit the mold?*

You can honor your roots without staying rooted in them.

PRACTICE

This week, try this:

- *Name one inherited message you're ready to examine— something about worth, behavior, strength, success, or identity.*
- *Then ask: Do I actually believe this? Or did I just absorb it?*
- *Next, choose one small way to live a little more aligned with who you are now—not who you were expected to be.*

That might mean speaking up where you'd usually go quiet, changing a routine that no longer serves you, or admitting that something you were taught doesn't work for you anymore

Alignment doesn't erase your story. It lets you tell it with your whole voice.

CHAPTER 14
WHEN THE PAYCHECK
ISN'T ENOUGH

I'VE HAD a lot of jobs.

When I was a freshman in college, a bunch of my friends and I decided to apply at a call center near campus. The ad promised flexible hours and easy money. We were told it wasn't "sales"—we'd just be enrolling people in a free radio contest. What that meant, exactly, I wasn't sure. There had to be some kind of fine print involved, but I was twenty, from the farm, and didn't ask a lot of questions. I just wanted a paycheck.

After the training session, we were sent to our desks to make our first round of calls. I picked up the headset, read the script, and dialed exactly three numbers before I knew: this wasn't it. I hated that I was using a fake name. I hated the cold-calling and hated talking to strangers who were irritated about being bothered.

When my first break came, I slipped out, got in my car, and drove away. I never went back. No dramatic exit. Just... gone.

That was the first time I remember trusting the part of me that said, "This isn't for you."

Since then, I've worked all kinds of jobs. I sold TVs at Best Buy and Bibles at Berean Christian Store. I pushed carts at Walmart and helped people lease apartments. I managed the office of a Methodist church, ran tech support back when dial-up internet still whined through the walls, and sat through more than one budget meeting as an Associate Director in a nonprofit agency.

In every one of those roles, I learned things. There were parts I liked, parts I endured, and parts that taught me—sometimes slowly, sometimes immediately—what I wasn't built for.

But across all of them, one theme always emerged: I'm at my best when I'm helping people.

Not in a vague, save-the-world kind of way. I just feel most like myself when I'm showing up for someone in real time—using what I've learned to offer clarity, or comfort, or truth. I don't mind the paperwork, the logistics, the behind-the-scenes chaos—if it's in service of something meaningful. If it connects. If it matters.

As a therapist, I've worked in non-profits, group practices, hospitals, and now in private practice. I've trained others, supervised teams, presented workshops, and handled alarm codes and audit protocols. Some of those jobs were aligned with who I was at the time. Others weren't.

But private practice? This feels right. Not because it's perfect—but because it's mine. Because the work reflects my values. Because I'm not pretending.

I'm not hustling to be impressive. I'm just working in a space that fits.

This is another example of what alignment looks like.

WHEN THE DREAM ISN'T YOURS

Amber's parents brought her to therapy because she had stopped going to practice.

This was not a minor issue in their household. Amber had been training as a gymnast since before she could write her name. Her schedule was structured around competitions, conditioning, and coaching sessions. Her walls were lined with medals. Her social life—what little there was —consisted of teammates and travel meets. This wasn't just a hobby. It was a trajectory. Her parents had poured time, money, and identity into her potential. The Olympics weren't guaranteed, but they were the goal. Everyone in her world knew it.

Except Amber.

She hadn't quit outright. She just... started missing things. Sleeping in. Skipping strength training. Faking injuries. Then came the panic attacks. The insomnia. The sense that she was watching her life like a movie she didn't remember auditioning for.

She was sixteen when they brought her to me. Tall, lean, strong. Her posture was perfect. Her tone was polite. Her smile was practiced. She'd been taught to perform—even in conversation. But there was something underneath. A quiet heaviness.

Her parents framed the issue clearly: she was "losing motivation." She was "acting out." She was "throwing away her future."

She hadn't told them yet what she told me in our second session.

"I don't want this," she said. "I never did. I want to be a nurse like my aunt. I want to go to school and help people. Not flip around in front of a panel of judges."

She looked at me like she was confessing something shameful. Like she was letting me down, too.

But I didn't see laziness. I didn't see rebellion. I saw a girl waking up. A girl realizing she had a body—and a voice—and that both were hers to protect.

Amber didn't hate gymnastics. She hated that her worth had been tied to her performance. That her usefulness had become her identity. That her entire value as a daughter—as a person—had been measured in placements and rankings and podiums.

She didn't want to be rescued. She just wanted to stop disappointing everyone by telling the truth.

I didn't tell her what to do. But I asked her what it would feel like to live a life that was hers. One where the hard work she put in wasn't about making other people proud—it was about showing up for something she actually believed in.

She started shadowing her aunt at a local clinic. She volunteered on weekends. Her posture started to shift—not from perfection, but from purpose. She still did gymnastics for a while, but on her terms. Eventually, she stopped altogether. She applied to nursing school. She got in.

Her parents were disappointed. Maybe they still are.

But Amber? She's not.

She found a way to be useful without being used.

And that's the difference.

QUICK CHECK-IN: WORK, WORTH, AND WHY

Take a minute and ask yourself:

- *What parts of your work feel aligned with who you really are?*
- *What do you love about what you do—not just tolerate?*
- *Where are you performing a version of usefulness that no longer fits?*
- *Who taught you what "success" should look like?*
- *What might change if you stopped trying to prove your worth through your work?*

You don't have to bleed for your calling. You just have to be honest about what's calling you.

THE WORK THAT FITS

Amber found a path that resonated with her soul, despite other people's expectations of her. I didn't have Olympic pressure on my shoulders, but I know what it's like to let my identity get tangled in other people's expectations.

And somewhere along the way, I started asking myself the same question she had—maybe not in words, but in spirit: Who gets to decide what makes a life meaningful?

For a long time, I assumed meaningful work had to be exhausting. That it had to look selfless. That it had to involve late nights, personal sacrifice, and a kind of noble suffering that proved you were all in. I believed you had to earn your calling by bleeding for it a little. Especially in helping professions. Especially when your value came from being needed.

I don't believe that anymore.

Meaningful work isn't about how impressive your résumé sounds or how many letters trail behind your name. I once had a professor whose credentials ran the full length of his business card—line after line of degrees and certifications. When I asked what they all meant, he looked at me and said, without missing a beat: "It means I have low self-esteem, Kirk."

I've never forgotten that.

Because sometimes the hardest work isn't the kind we do in an office or a clinic or a classroom. It's the work of asking ourselves: Why am I doing this? Who am I trying to impress? What am I hoping this role or title will finally prove about me?

Meaningful work doesn't come from proving your worth. It comes from remembering you already have it.

It's about whether or not it aligns with who you are.

It's about whether your values, your voice, your actual self gets to show up in the work—not just the version of you that keeps the donors happy or the board satisfied or the clients calm.

Meaningful work can look like teaching. Or therapy. Or artistry. Or accounting. Or raising a child. Or running a bookstore. It can be quiet. It can be ordinary. It can be seasonal. And sometimes, it doesn't look like "work" at all—not in the capitalist sense. Sometimes the most aligned work you'll ever do won't come with a paycheck.

But what it will come with is a sense of integrity.

You'll stop feeling like you're selling your soul just to clock in. You'll stop fantasizing about quitting during every lunch break. You'll stop imagining a different life—because you've already started building one that fits.

EXTRA WHIPPED CREAM

I don't understand networking events. I've had more meaningful connections over pancakes at 3 a.m. than I have at any professional or work gathering. Someone looking me in the eye, getting my order right, and calling me by name means more than any business card exchange I've had.

A few years ago, I was a regular at the 24-hour IHOP near my apartment. It wasn't fancy. The lighting was harsh, the tables were a little sticky, and the food always tasted better the later it got. But it was open when I needed it to be. And Victoria worked the overnight shift.

I didn't know much about her, and she didn't know much about me. But she knew that I liked to drink Mountain Dew. She knew I preferred Swiss cheese on my burgers, and that sometimes I ordered fries, sometimes onion rings. I knew she was in college and working third shift to get through it. So maybe we knew more about each other than we thought.

One night, as she dropped off my plate, she said, "I guess I might as well tell you now... tonight's my last night here."

It caught me off guard. I didn't even know her last name. But I felt a lump in my throat.

She started to confide in me—told me the general manager hadn't treated her well. I empathized, and then I made a joke. "Well, who's going to take care of me?"

It wasn't totally sincere, but I meant it. She made the place feel safe. Like it was okay to be alone at 3 a.m. and still feel known.

The next time I went back, Victoria was gone. The place felt... off. The kitchen was understaffed. The manager was back there cooking. Orders were taking forever. They were out of pancakes—at a place where pancake was in their name.

It wasn't just that Victoria provided quality service. It was about atmosphere. Presence. Care.

I missed her.

And that's when I realized: even casual relationships matter. Even when they're simple. Even when you barely know the person's last name. Presence matters. Dignity matters. Being seen—even by someone who's paid to be there—can shift your whole day.

Betty Jo reminds me of that, too.

I met her at one of those chain diners that still feels local. She greeted me from across the room like I was a regular, even though I wasn't. She called me by name every time she passed the table. She got my vanilla Coke refilled over and over without me having to ask. She asked about dessert, put extra whipped cream on my pumpkin pie, then brought my check with a note attached: *Shine Your Light.*

That little Post-it said more than any corporate mission statement.

I've been back to that diner nearly every week since. I always request Betty Jo—because frankly, I don't go there for the food.

Betty Jo didn't give me a TED Talk on customer service. She wasn't chasing a metric. She just did her thing—and fabulously, I should add. She made me feel like I mattered—like I wasn't just a check number or a time slot. She turned a meal into something kind.

I remember those moments more vividly than a lot of the jobs I've had. Because when someone does their work with integrity and presence, you feel it. Not because it's glamorous or groundbreaking. But because it honors the human on the other end of the interaction.

It's not always about changing the world. Sometimes it's about changing the atmosphere of a booth with extra whipped cream.

SOUL AUDIT: Work & Calling

Your work doesn't have to be your whole identity. But if it's misaligned, it can cost you more than time—it can cost you your sense of self.

Check all that apply:

- ☐ I've stayed in roles that drained me because they looked "right" on paper
- ☐ I confuse being productive with being valuable
- ☐ I've ignored my inner "this isn't it" to avoid rocking the boat
- ☐ **I've felt most like myself doing work that isn't on my résumé**
- ☐ **I believe meaningful work doesn't have to mean misery**
- ☐ **I'm beginning to imagine work that fits—not just pays**

If any of these landed with you, take a moment.

What is your work *costing* you? What is it *offering* you?

You don't have to love every task. But you deserve to feel like you belong to yourself—even on the clock.

Work should fit your soul—not force it into a costume.

FROM THE AUDIT TO ACTION

Awareness

Work doesn't have to be your whole identity.

But if it costs you your peace, your health, or your dignity—it's not neutral, either.

Ask yourself:

- *Where in your life do you feel most alive when you're contributing?*
- *Where do you feel most invisible or drained?*
- *If you didn't have to impress anyone, what kind of work would you actually want to do—or create?*

Your calling doesn't have to be flashy. It just has to be yours.

Practice

This week, let yourself daydream on purpose.

Imagine one "tiny career rebellion" you could take—something that would bring you back toward yourself.

(Examples: saying no to a pointless meeting, taking a lunch break without guilt, sketching out a side project that lights you up.)

Or:

Write a "wanted ad" for the kind of work you crave—not the kind you think you're allowed to want.

(Example: "Wanted: Work that lets me think deeply, move slowly, and be useful without disappearing.")

Work matters. But so does how you feel while you're doing it.

CHAPTER 15
WE HAD A PLAN

THERE ARE two kinds of people in this world: those who wing it—and those who build a spreadsheet with color-coded tabs.

I am the spreadsheet.

Especially when I'm going to Disney World.

Before the trip even begins, I've already created a rainbow-coded document that outlines our park schedule, Genie+ ride reservations, dinner reservations, park hours, and confirmation numbers for every aspect of the trip. I hyperlink menus. I color-coordinate wait times. I build contingency plans. It's not a hobby—it's a calling.

And no one respects my calling more than Dr. Cheryl Campbell.

You'll hear a lot about her in this chapter, because she's been my co-pilot on more adventures than anyone else. We've known each other for two decades, but our friendship really solidified when we discovered our mutual love for Walt Disney World. She's a retired psychologist, a master of quiet independence, and the only person I ever want to travel with.

She also defers entirely to my planning. She lets me build the trip down to the minute. I get up early to make our reservations. I handle mobile ordering. I manage our Lightning Lane strategy like it's a military operation. She follows the itinerary with the kind of loyalty most people reserve for court orders.

But even with all the planning in the world, there are always surprises.

Because the thing about life—and especially travel—is that it rarely sticks to the itinerary.

And as you'll soon see, some of the best stories Cheryl and I have collected together didn't come from what worked.

They came from what fell apart.

THE DOCTOR WILL DINE NOW

Cheryl usually lets me make the reservations. But one night, she booked dinner for us at California Grill.

It's one of Disney's fanciest restaurants—on the top floor of the Contemporary Resort with panoramic views of Magic Kingdom and a front-row seat to the fireworks. The kind of place where the sushi is exceptional, the lighting is dim, and the prices suggest you're paying as much for altitude as ambiance.

She'd made the reservation online and—out of habit or perhaps professionalism—used her full name: Dr. Cheryl Campbell.

When we arrived and checked in at the podium, the host looked at the screen, smiled warmly, and said, "Ah! Good evening, Dr. Campbell. Right this way."

Cheryl's face didn't move. But I saw the twitch in her eyebrow. And I knew instantly: this was going to be a thing.

For the record, she doesn't go around calling herself Dr. Campbell. She earned the title—PhD in psychology—but she only uses it with attorneys, or when she needs to be taken seriously in a professional setting.

Never on airplanes (in case someone goes into labor), and certainly not on vacation.

But our server leaned into the formality like she was auditioning for a Victorian period drama.

She addressed Cheryl as "Doctor" every time she approached the table. And for some reason, she referred to me as "Mr. Kirk," like I was a concierge at a retirement community.

The tone was so crisp—so performatively deferential—that it felt less like a dinner reservation and more like a dissertation defense.

I tried to lighten the mood. We both started referring to each other by ridiculous honorifics.

"Doctor, are you enjoying your filet mignon?"

"Indeed, Mister Kirk, it is exquisite."

"Thank you, your majesty."

"You're welcome, your lordship."

And so on.

The food was spectacular. The view was stunning. The fireworks happened right on cue.

But something about the evening felt... off. A little too formal. A little too stilted. We couldn't relax.

And I realized: it's not just about the food or the view. It's about how you feel in the space. Whether you can take a deep breath, or whether you feel like you're still in costume.

Sometimes misalignment doesn't scream. It whispers. It's a tightness in your shoulders. A slight shift in your tone. A voice in your head asking, *Why do I feel like I'm pretending right now?*

We finished our meal, tipped generously, and left feeling... fine. It was good. But not the kind of good that lingers. Not the kind that becomes a favorite.

Alignment doesn't just show up in how something looks. It shows up in how you feel in your own skin.

And the moment someone calls you by a name you don't recognize—even if it's technically correct—you start to feel the seams of the performance tug a little.

THE YARIS INCIDENT

It's not only Disney where things can go awry.

Cheryl and I once decided to drive to Little Rock to see our friend DJ perform in "The Little Mermaid." The plan was simple: split the cost of a rental car, take our time getting there, stop somewhere near Nashville for the night, and roll into Arkansas fresh and well-rested. Simple. Smart. Sensible.

Until we met the Yaris.

We'd booked a compact car—something fuel-efficient and affordable. I thought the rental clerk said "Taurus," which would have been perfectly acceptable. Cheryl thought she said "TARDIS," which would've been a tight fit but a heck of a good time (though I've still never seen an entire episode of *Doctor Who*).

What we actually got was a Toyota Yaris, which is basically a motorized lunchbox.

For Cheryl, who is petite, this wasn't a huge issue. For me—six-foot-three-and-two-thirds inches tall and occupying what most airlines would call a "comfort plus seat and then some"—it was less than ideal. I folded myself into the passenger seat like origami, knees pressed against the dash, trying not to think about how many more hours we had ahead of us.

Still, we were in good spirits. I was in charge of the playlist, shuffling between comedy clips and Beatles deep cuts. We had snacks. We had caffeine. We were on our way.

Until we hit Louisville.

Or more accurately: we didn't hit Louisville. Because traffic stopped. Not slowed—stopped. Four lanes of unmoving, brake-light-stained gridlock with no exit in sight.

And just as the car came to a dead halt, Cheryl turned to me with wide eyes and said, "I have to pee."

Not in a casual way. Not in a "Hey, remind me next time we stop" kind of way. In a this-is-an-emergency kind of way.

There was nothing I could do. I didn't offer encouragement. I didn't make calming noises. I didn't say helpful things like, "Maybe it's just a phantom urge" or "Surely we're almost through." I just held on and hoped for the best.

Cheryl gripped the steering wheel like we were on the autobahn. Her patience began to dissolve. Her mood shifted from tense to homicidal. Every driver around us became the enemy. Every family station wagon, every SUV, every motorcycle—we hated them all.

And I, knowing better than to add fuel to the fire, continued to say nothing.

Eventually—*eventually*—we made it through the worst of it and spotted an Arby's off the first available exit. Cheryl didn't park the car so much as launch it into a space. She yanked the gear shift into park, flung open the door, and sprinted for the bathroom with the kind of urgency usually reserved for medical dramas and Olympic trials.

I sat in the car, unsure if I should pray or text DJ to say we might not make it.

A few minutes later, she returned. She didn't speak for a moment. Then, deadpan and dignified, she buckled her seatbelt and said:

"Next time, I'm wearing Depends."

You can't plan for everything—but you can *dress* for it.

THE COST OF CHEAP

We thought we could just find a place off the highway.

That was the plan, anyway. After escaping Louisville traffic and surviving the Great Bladder Emergency, we figured we'd stop somewhere outside Nashville for the night. Nothing fancy. Just a clean bed, a working lock, and a place to regroup before heading to Little Rock the next day.

Then we saw the glowing red sign: **Rooms – $49.00**

It practically screamed: "You'll regret this, but only slightly." We pulled in.

The man at the desk handed us our keys like he was passing off evidence. The lobby smelled like old coffee and stale mop water. But it was late, we were tired, and I figured if we died, someone would at least be able to track our phones.

We requested two rooms—always separate rooms. We like each other, but not that much—and headed off to opposite sides of the hallway. My room had an air conditioner that sounded like it was trying to take off. There were two mismatched lamps and a bedspread that looked like it had survived several presidential administrations. But it was technically a bed. I got under the covers fully clothed, watched something forgettable on my iPad, and passed out.

When I woke up the next morning, I felt pretty pleased with myself. I had survived the $49 motel. Not bad. I gathered my things and made my way to the lobby, already imagining the fast-food breakfast I was going to order.

That's when Cheryl looked at me with stone-cold intensity and said, "Go wait in the car."

I didn't ask questions. I just went.

A few minutes later, she got in the car and stared ahead at the dashboard.

"So," she said, "around midnight, there was a loud knock on my door. The manager said there were noise complaints coming from my room. He told me if I didn't quiet down, he'd throw me out."

She hadn't been loud. She hadn't done anything.

She'd been watching TV in bed, like any other adult in a budget motel trying to mind her business and not get lice. The volume was low. There were no phone calls. No music. Just Cheryl. In silence. Trying to relax.

And yet, here was a man banging on her door in the middle of the night, threatening to evict her like she was a rowdy spring breaker throwing a party. He wouldn't let her ask questions. Wouldn't explain the complaint. Just kept repeating himself and walking away. She barely slept after that.

She didn't want me to see her lose it when she complained—or maybe she was afraid I'd lose it had I knew what happened to her (highly likely) but I knew when she said to "wait in the car" that there was no choice to be made.

The morning manager was very apologetic and comped both of our rooms. But the damage was already done. Cheryl isn't someone who gets rattled easily—but she was thrown, for sure.

It wasn't about the room. Or the man. Or even the threat.

It was about being accused of something she didn't do. About the deep, disorienting feeling of not being safe somewhere that was supposed to be a place of rest.

We got breakfast. Cheryl unwrapped her sandwich like she was performing a surgery. She barely touched her food. And before we pulled out of the parking lot, looked across the street at the glowing $49 discount sign, she said, "We're not doing that again."

And we haven't.

Sometimes alignment is just deciding you're no longer available for anything that threatens your peace. Even if it's cheap. Even if it's convenient. Even if it's only for one night.

NEVER AGAIN

Speaking of never doing that again...

One summer, Cheryl and I made our annual pilgrimage to Cedar Point —America's Roller Coast—and decided to take a scenic detour to the Marblehead Lighthouse.

It was a beautiful day. Sunny. Breezy. The kind of weather that tricks you into thinking you're invincible. The admission was three dollars. Cheryl paid mine before I could object.

The Marblehead Lighthouse is charming from the ground. From the top, it's a death trap designed by someone with sado-masochistic tendencies and an open grudge against people with a fear of heights. The stairs were metal. Grated. Spiral. See-through. There was one flimsy handrail and nothing else between you and the open abyss of a very permanent fall.

I have a longstanding fear of heights. Not a vague discomfort. A full-bodied, sweaty-palmed, I-might-die-here kind of fear. Add in the fact that I'm not exactly small and the spiral staircase was narrower than most theme park turnstiles, and you've got the ingredients for a personal disaster.

But Cheryl had already paid, and I didn't want to seem ungrateful. So I went.

I used both sides of the stairwell to climb, hands pressed against metal like I was scaling a prison tower. I tried to stay calm. Breathe. Pretend this wasn't a mistake.

At the top, I tried to enjoy the view. Lake Erie stretched out in every direction. The sky was crisp. It didn't matter; I couldn't breathe and I just wanted down.

And then I heard it: a child. Screaming.

He was on the stairs. Refusing to go up or down. Just standing there, paralyzed with fear and determination. His mother was pleading with him. I could hear the frustration in her voice. But the kid wasn't budging.

I wasn't either.

Because now, we were stuck.

Eventually, I made the executive decision to descend. Slowly. Carefully. One step at a time, using my freakishly long arms to grip both walls as I crept downward like a cautious crab.

That's when I heard Cheryl's voice behind me.

"Kirk."

That's all she said. But it was *how* she said it.

Cheryl only uses my first name like that when something is very wrong.

I turned back. She was frozen at the top, white-knuckling the railing, eyes wide with panic. She wasn't okay.

She said, "I don't think I can do this."

I offered encouragement. But I didn't offer to go back up and help. I didn't offer to carry her, which, in retrospect, would've created an even bigger emergency.

Eventually, she scooted.

One step at a time, sitting on her butt like a toddler at a playground slide, Cheryl bumped her way down the entire spiral staircase. I stayed in front, ready to catch her or at least break her fall, or something. I don't know.

We passed the still-screaming child and his exhausted mother on the landing. I gave them a sympathetic nod, but didn't slow down. We were focused. Mission: Survive.

When we got to the bottom, we stood in silence for a few seconds. Then Cheryl turned to me and said, "If I ever try to do that again, please remind me of this moment."

I assured her I would. Loudly. And often.

Cheryl didn't scoot down those stairs because she wanted to prove something. She did it because it was the only way forward. It wasn't graceful. It wasn't dignified. But it was the path that worked. And sometimes, that's the most aligned move you can make—scooting down one step at a time, owning your fear, choosing presence over performance.

QUICK CHECK-IN: SCOOTING TOWARD ALIGNMENT

Not every step forward has to be graceful. Sometimes alignment looks like scooting—awkward, slow, honest. Sometimes it's just choosing not to freeze, not to fake it, not to pretend you're fine.

Take a moment. Then ask yourself:

- *What's something I've was scared of but did anyway?*
- *Where in my life do I feel stuck between "freezing" and "moving"?*
- *Who's been willing to sit with me—or scoot with me—when things got hard?*
- *What would it look like to take one forward step right now, even if it's not elegant?*

You don't have to soar. You just have to keep scooting.

WE CAME FOR A SHOW

We'd driven a long way to see our friend Tyler perform in *Hairspray*.

The theatre was outdoors—in the middle of the woods at Jenny Wiley State Park in eastern Kentucky. No roof. No backup plan. Just a stage, some lights, and the hope that the weather would hold.

We didn't know exactly what we were walking into. The place was remote, the forecast wasn't promising, and the kind of magic live theatre requires doesn't always survive bad weather and bad acoustics. But we loved Tyler. And we came ready to support him.

On the drive we passed the Ark Encounter. We passed Red River Gorge. We wound our way through small towns and tree-lined roads, slowly climbing toward the state park lodge. We'd booked separate rooms, as always. It was nothing fancy—just somewhere to sleep after the show— but better than a $49 room outside of Nashville.

We had a brief moment of panic at check-in when the clerk couldn't find both reservations. I imagined the two of us stuck in a room with one queen bed and a view of a dumpster. But all was resolved. We dropped our bags, refreshed ourselves, and got ready to meet Tyler for dinner.

The town was small, but we found a little gem of a restaurant—a place called The Brick House. It was in, well, a brick house. During dinner, Tyler gave us the inside scoop. The cast was talented. Rehearsals had been tight. But there'd been some tension, too. Especially after a group of Black cast members had been confronted while walking into town.

"Someone asked why they were here," Tyler said.

It wasn't friendly curiosity. It was suspicion. *That* kind of suspicion.

The director had talked to the cast about how *Hairspray*—a show about integration and acceptance—was particularly important to perform in a community like this. Still, it added a layer of caution. Of weight. Of purpose.

We dropped Tyler off backstage and made our way to the amphitheater. The sky was already threatening us with clouds and mist. I had my umbrella ready, just in case.

The show began. It drizzled. The cast performed anyway.

They danced and sang through *Good Morning Baltimore* with all the energy of a full house, even though the audience was maybe fifty people in a venue built for ten times that. There was no cover, no backup plan. Just grit and talent and hope.

Partway through the first act, the rain started coming down harder.

Then the sky cracked.

A bolt of lightning hit something behind the stage. There was a massive boom. And then smoke.

We didn't know it yet, but a transformer had blown and started a fire in the woods. The show was immediately stopped. Cheryl and I made a run for it, umbrellas flailing.

We ducked into the lodge lobby, along with the cast, the crew, and the scattered audience members who hadn't already evacuated.

Half the building had lost power. The bar was closed. People were wet and annoyed. Others were laughing. The energy was all over the place.

And then, something shifted.

Without a cue, a small group of the Black cast members gathered near the entrance. One of them started to sing. No microphone. No introduction.

Just that first line:

There's a light in the darkness...

It was *I Know Where I've Been.* The act two big number. Usually a showstopper. This time, it was an *everything-stopper.*

A cappella. Softly at first. Then with power.

The room fell silent.

Even the annoyed wet guy in cargo shorts put his phone away.

And there, in the half-lit lobby of a lodge in the middle of nowhere, surrounded by rain and smoke and the smell of soggy socks and wet hair, we all stood still. Listening.

The woman singing lead had tears in her eyes. So did I. So did Cheryl. The notes wrapped around us like a blanket. There was no stage. No lights. No choreography.

Just truth. Deep, beautiful truth.

And that's the moment I'll remember. Not the near-crisis with the rooms. Not the weather. Not even the fire.

The unscripted, sacred moment when *something real* broke through all the chaos and said, "This matters."

We came to see a show. We found a benediction.

AFTER THE SPREADSHEET

I don't think any of these stories would've made the spreadsheet.

- Not the Depends declaration.
- Not the haunted motel with its imaginary noise complaints.
- Not the lighthouse meltdown.
- And certainly not the lobby fire-and-rainstorm finale.

None of it was planned. All of it mattered.

This chapter was supposed to be about control. About how I love it. About how Cheryl lets me have it. About how our best adventures usually happen *right after* it falls apart.

It turns out, alignment doesn't always look like confidence. Or organization. Or leadership. Sometimes, it looks like scooting down a spiral staircase on your butt.

Sometimes, it looks like standing still in a lodge lobby, drenched and stunned, while strangers sing something that breaks your heart wide open.

And sometimes, it looks like waving to a crowd of strangers from a popcorn-themed pedicab in a T-shirt two sizes too small.

THE POPCORN PARADE PRINCIPLE

After our Marble Head Lighthouse Trauma, Cheryl and I didn't ascend any more towers. I wouldn't even the use the stairs in Hotel Breakers.

But we *did* climb onto a popcorn-themed parade float at Cedar Point thanks to Cheryl's engagement with a stranger with a clipboard.

It was hot. Like stand-still-and-sweat hot. Cheryl and I were parked on a bench trying to decide how to pass the time without passing out. We'd spent the earlier part of the day traversing the park, and even Cheryl—who has what often feels like a limitless well of energy—was content to sit still for a bit.

But she was also getting bored.

That's when two employees from the marketing team strolled by holding a sign that said, "Want to be a Grand Marshal?"

Without hesitation, Cheryl shouted, "Sure!"

They turned. "Do you have two more friends? We need a group of four."

Cheryl immediately started advocating for our friends Jeff and Nicole and their two kids, who were back at the hotel. Unfortunately, there was no way they could make it in time. So, she asked them again if we could do it. They pushed back, saying they really needed a party of four. We jokingly protested, citing discrimination against twofers. They were unmoved, or that's what we thought.

We laughed it off, thanked the staffers, and settled back into our sweaty state of non-motion.

Five minutes later, one of the guys came back.

"I know we said no," he said, "but we found another group of two... so..."

Before he could finish the sentence, we were nodding emphatically and possibly clapping.

He left to get our VIP wristbands and told us to meet him at the giant "150 Years" sign at the park's entrance. From there, we'd get our photo taken and be escorted *backstage* to load into a pedicab—our very own parade float for the evening.

I looked at Cheryl. She looked at me. We were stunned. And thrilled.

"This is why you talk to people," she said, not subtly.

She was right, of course. I often whisper *"Disengage"* under my breath when she starts chatting up strangers in line. Sometimes she listens. Sometimes she doubles down. And sometimes—like this—we end up becoming grand marshals in a theme park parade.

Our photos were taken. Jeremy from Entertainment came to escort us backstage. He handed us T-shirts and explained the rules. No photos behind the scenes. Smile like we belonged. Wave like it mattered.

There were two float themes: popcorn and cotton candy. We were given the first pick. Popcorn it was.

For the record, the T-shirts were XLs. I haven't worn an XL since, oh, the Bush administration. The first one. But I squeezed myself in, arms barely mobile, ready for whatever came next.

We climbed into the pedicab, our driver Bekka full of energy and encouragement. "You're gonna love this," she said. "You'll be stars."

I apologized for making her haul my plus-sized adult body through the park. She laughed and assured me she'd done worse.

Backstage, a performer in full costume announced it was "Christmas in July." We all sang a modified version of *Sleigh Ride* using the word *float* instead of *sleigh*. Spirits were high. No one was too cool to be there. It was beautiful.

Taylor—possibly the choreographer—checked in on us. Everyone seemed genuinely glad we were there. And then, just like that, the music started, and the parade began.

We were rolled through the streets of Cedar Point, waving like pageant queens, smiling like local celebrities. Some park guests looked confused, as if wondering whether we were famous and they just didn't recognize us. That only made me wave harder.

We hit three separate "dance break" stops where the performers gave their all. Then we were dropped off at a VIP viewing area for the end-of-night stage show. They led us right to the front.

It was incredible. These performers had just danced the full parade route and now were giving a Broadway-level finale under hot lights with full commitment. I'd seen some of them earlier in the day in other shows. They hadn't lost a single step.

I turned to Cheryl at one point and said, "This is the closest I'll ever get to being in a theme park show."

She nodded. "But we got here. Somehow."

We didn't plan this moment. We didn't earn it through effort or connections. We just said yes.

Sometimes alignment doesn't come from striving. It comes from staying open. Saying "sure" when someone walks by with a clipboard. Letting yourself be seen. Letting joy be enough.

There was no career boost from this. No deep personal breakthrough. Just two sweaty weirdos in popcorn-themed shirts, waving to strangers like it meant something.

And maybe that's the point. Maybe alignment isn't always about what you do—but how willing you are to say yes.

Even if it means squeezing into a shirt two sizes too small.

CONTROL IS NOT THE GOAL

We joke about being control freaks. How we plan everything to the minute and make color-coded itineraries and backup plans for our backup plans. It's endearing and funny. Until it isn't.

Because underneath control is usually fear. Underneath the spreadsheet is a story. And sometimes, the grip we keep on the wheel is the very thing making the ride so bumpy.

Annette came into session tense. Her neck was stiff. Her body tight. Her energy buzzing just beneath the surface. She told me about the upcoming shift at work—how two coworkers were taking the day off, how they would be short-staffed, how she'd have to jump in, manage chaos, take phone calls, cover lunches, train new people. "I was so worked up," she said. "Full of fear and anxiety. I was spiraling."

She woke up the next morning in physical pain. Her anxiety had become a body experience. And the worst part? Friday turned out fine.

"Once again," she said, "I wasn't in control of my fear or anxiety. I kept trying to talk myself out of it—telling myself I knew what I was doing. But it didn't work."

That's when we started to unpack what was *really* happening.

"My go-to when I feel anxious," she said, "is to squash it. Control it. Pretend it's not there. Beat it down."

177

"What if the control," I asked, "is what's making it worse?"

We talked about a new approach—not managing anxiety like a problem to solve, but meeting it like an old friend. "Hello, anxiety. Thanks for reminding me to be conscientious and prepared. But I don't need you to take over today. You can come along, but you're not in charge."

She nodded slowly. "So it's not about making it go away. It's about coexisting with it?"

Exactly. Because her anxiety wasn't the enemy. It's what made her excellent at her job. It's what made her thoughtful and on time. But when she tried to *control* it, she actually fed it.

We talked about mindfulness, about journaling, about putting her thoughts on trial: "What would a reasonable jury of your peers say about this fear?" She liked that image. It made her feel less alone.

Then she brought up something else.

"The phone thing again," she said.

A friend had texted her: "I want to call you today."

Annette's immediate reaction was to text back: "I'm busy. I can't."

"Why?" I asked.

"I don't know. It just freaked me out."

"Were you afraid you were in trouble?"

"Maybe. Or that she'd hear something in my voice. Or I'd say something wrong. Or I wouldn't have anything to say."

Phone calls, we realized, felt too intimate. Too unscripted. Too vulnerable.

And that's what this was all really about.

Not just control. Not just anxiety. But vulnerability.

We want to control our feelings because we're afraid of being exposed. Of not being prepared. Of being seen.

Annette went deeper.

She talked about her mom and dad. About how she grew up thinking she had to manage her emotions—her anger, her sadness, her fear. "I thought I needed to learn how to *control* them," she said, "because they were controlling me."

She paused. Then she said something I'll never forget:

"I think I figured out a long time ago that the only way to stay safe in my family—and in the world—was to control everything. I controlled the narrative. I hid parts of myself. I stayed ahead of the feelings so they wouldn't catch up to me."

She looked up at me. "But it doesn't work anymore. I don't need it anymore."

Control had kept her safe. Until it didn't.

And now she was learning a new way to be.

Before we ended, she landed on a mantra: *Control is not the goal.*

We say it often now. It reminds her that alignment doesn't come from perfect execution. It comes from presence. From acceptance. From practicing a new relationship with her feelings.

Control isn't always the villain. It's often a protector. But if we never update the job description, it becomes a tyrant.

The goal isn't to eliminate anxiety. The goal is to *move with it.*

The goal isn't to avoid hard feelings. It's to *coexist* with them.

The goal, always, is alignment.

SOUL AUDIT: PLANNING AND CONTROL

Planning offers structure. But control is different—it masquerades as safety, while quietly disconnecting us from the moment we're in.

Check all that apply:

- ☐ I get anxious when plans change—even if the outcome still works out
- ☐ I plan to feel secure, but I rarely feel settled
- ☐ I have a hard time relaxing unless I'm in charge
- ☐ **Some of my best moments weren't planned—and they surprised me**
- ☐ **I'm learning to let go of how it "should" go and notice what's actually happening**
- ☐ **I trust myself more than I trust my to-do list**

If any of this feels familiar, take a breath. You're not doing it wrong. You're just learning to loosen the grip.

Control might feel like safety—but presence is what helps you feel at home in your own life.

You don't have to let go of the plan entirely. Just let it breathe.

Let *yourself* breathe.

FROM THE AUDIT TO ACTION

Awareness

Planning is a gift. But control? That's something else. When control becomes a coping strategy, it can keep us from being present in the very moments we worked so hard to prepare for.

Ask yourself:

- *Where am I clinging to control, hoping it will keep me safe—or successful?*
- *What moments am I missing because I'm too focused on managing them?*
- *Where do I confuse structure with security?*
- *What would it feel like to let go of how it's supposed to be—and just let it be?*

The moment doesn't have to be perfect to be meaningful.

PRACTICE

This week, let one thing be unscripted. Don't over-plan it. Don't rehearse your lines. Just show up.

If it goes "wrong," ask yourself: *Did something else show up that mattered more?*

Practice noticing: *What do I feel when things go off-plan?*

And more importantly: *What do I discover when I stay in the moment anyway?*

Alignment isn't about perfection. It's about presence. Let the plan serve you—not the other way around.

CHAPTER 16
THE BODY DOESN'T LIE

CHERYL and I arrived at Disney's Hollywood Studios right at park opening. The air buzzed with anticipation—it was the first Star Wars Weekend of the year, back when that was still a thing. Stormtroopers were perched above the entrance, mocking guests below. Everyone surged toward the left side of the park where all the Star Wars merchandise and meet-and-greets were happening.

Not me. I went right. Straight to the Twilight Zone Tower of Terror.

She and I had come together, but Cheryl was all-in on the Star Wars festivities. I, on the other hand, had my own ritual: head to the most atmospheric, thematically brilliant ride in the park while everyone else was distracted. Alone. No lines. Just me, the ghosts of a fictional 1930s hotel, and the smell of fake dust and old velvet.

I walked through the cobwebbed lobby, straight into the boiler room, and was ushered to an open elevator. There was no one else. I was getting a zen ride—coaster enthusiast slang for when you ride something completely alone.

I buckled in, already grinning. The elevator rose. The eerie lighting flickered. The screen crackled to life with a Rod Serling monologue about the night the hotel guests vanished. And then the drops began—fast, unpredictable, body-lifting drops that make you laugh and scream at the same time.

It was thrilling. Unexpected. Perfect. Unsettling to do it alone.

And completely curated.

I was strapped in, yes. I was falling, technically. But every inch of the experience had been designed for safety. For effect. For fun. My body trusted the ride because it knew the system had been built to hold me.

That hasn't always been true.

In pro wrestling, I spent over 20 years throwing my body around concrete floors, metal posts, and roped-off rings. I was lucky—I never had a major injury. But that doesn't mean I didn't feel the effects.

There was a spot I used to do where the babyface would chase me outside the ring. I'd run, look back, and smack face-first into the ring post before taking a comically dramatic bump onto the concrete. Sometimes it hurt. Sometimes it didn't. But every time, my body was the punchline.

One night, I took a fall off the ring apron and slammed the back of my head against the concrete. Roger Ruffen, my opponent that night, told me it sounded like an egg cracking. He rushed to check for blood. I was fine—or at least my skull was *intact*.

Another time, I fell off the ring apron and landed directly on my kneecap. To this day, I have a floating bursa sac that swells up every now and then to remind me the realities of this so-called fake sport.

My worst injury happened when WWE Superstar Karl Anderson—back then he was Chad 2 Badd—bailed on a dive where he was supposed to accidentally land on me. I leaned in to catch him, but he changed course, causing me to twist my knee. I could barely walk but still wrestled a full match the next day in Georgetown, Kentucky.

That's what we did. You worked through it. You finished the show. If you could stand, you could wrestle. The body was a tool. A prop. A means to an end.

But the body doesn't lie.

It carries truth long after we've convinced our minds to move on. It remembers the blows, the twists, the strain. Not just in wrestling, but in life.

The migraines that come after a week of people-pleasing. The tight shoulders after shrinking yourself in every room you enter. The upset stomach when you say yes to something that should've been a no.

Your body doesn't care about appearances. It's not performing. It's not trying to be good. It's just trying to tell you the truth.

That's what embodiment is. Not loving your body or fixing it—but living *in* it. Listening to it. Trusting that it knows what's true, even when your brain is trying to override it.

When I started listening to my body—not just silencing it—I realized how often I'd mistaken endurance for strength. Pushing through didn't make me powerful. It made me numb.

Now, I pay attention to the tension. I ask why I'm tired instead of blaming myself for being lazy. I notice when I flinch, when I brace, when I stop breathing. These aren't flaws. They're signals.

Alignment doesn't mean your body always feels good. But it does mean you stop assuming your body is lying.

That solo ride on the Tower of Terror? It was a thrill because I knew I was safe. I knew the system would catch me. I knew the fall wasn't real. Even doing it all alone.

But life doesn't always come with a seatbelt and a cast member in charge.

Sometimes the drop is real. Sometimes it hurts. And sometimes, the only way to find alignment again is to stop pretending you're fine and start listening to what your body has been trying to say all along.

It will tell you when it's time to rest. It will tell you when you're not safe. It will tell you when something isn't right.

The question is: will you listen?

I BELIEVE YOU

I used to think pain had to be dramatic to count. If you weren't bleeding, limping, or in a full-body cast, then you were probably fine. That's what I was taught, in ways both direct and implied. Real pain was visible. Verifiable. Something you could point to on an X-ray or get a prescription for. Everything else was "just stress" or "in your head."

Just "walk it off," right?

But over time—through therapy, personal experience, and paying attention—I've learned that some of the most debilitating pain doesn't show up in dramatic ways. It shows up in whispers. In fatigue that won't lift. In headaches that arrive like clockwork every Thursday afternoon after your staff meeting. In chronic inflammation, mystery ailments, and a collection of symptoms that get labeled as "unremarkable" in test results, but still wreck your ability to function.

There's a story in Oprah's book, *What Happened to You?*, that I've never forgotten. A young girl with Type 1 diabetes kept landing in the hospital with life-threatening spikes in blood sugar. Her doctors were stumped. Her food was monitored, her medication adjusted, but nothing seemed to make a difference.

Eventually, someone figured it out.

Every time she heard a siren—an ambulance—her blood sugar spiked. It wasn't something she was doing. It wasn't something she was eating. Her body was reacting to stored danger, to a traumatic memory tied to that sound. Not current danger. *Remembered* danger. Her mind didn't register it, but her body did. And her body responded as if the emergency was happening all over again.

That story stopped me in my tracks. Because I've seen the same thing in my work, more times than I can count.

Ruthie is one of those people. Not only did she have the hand injury, but other chronic physical ailments haunted her, too. Like chronic crippling migraines.

Her headaches didn't show up during stress. They arrived afterward—once she got home, once the tension dropped. Her body seemed to wait until the coast was clear to release the pain she'd been holding back all day. Her symptoms didn't follow a clean medical narrative. She had fatigue, brain fog, gut issues, and a general sense that her body had turned against her. Every test came back normal, but she didn't feel normal.

I didn't have a clinical diagnosis to offer to explain all of that. I wasn't there to explain or solve. But I could listen. And what I heard, again and again, was someone whose nervous system had been holding a survival posture for years—and was finally starting to exhale.

Getting medical professionals to listen was harder. And that kind of grief—the grief of being ignored, misunderstood, or dismissed—is its own wound. And it often takes the shape of pain that doesn't go away just because someone tells you it "shouldn't be there."

There's a scene in *The Golden Girls* where Dorothy spends months trying to get answers about her unrelenting fatigue. Doctors tell her it's nothing. That she's fine. That it's just anxiety. Eventually, she finds a specialist who gives her a name for what she's going through: Chronic Fatigue Syndrome. When he tells her he believes her, she cries from relief.

I remember that moment more vividly than I probably should. Because that's what validation feels like. Not just getting a label for your experience—but being seen. Being heard. Having someone look you in the eye and say, "I believe you."

Alignment is not about fixing every symptom or achieving perfect health. It's about stepping into a different kind of relationship with your body. A relationship where you don't assume the pain is a performance. A relationship where you trust that your body isn't exaggerating —it's communicating.

And when someone finally listens, when *you* finally listen, something shifts. Maybe not overnight. Maybe not dramatically. But slowly, steadily, something inside starts to exhale.

Your body isn't betraying you; it's trying to protect you.

LEARNING TO LISTEN

When you start paying attention to your body, it might feel like a betrayal. Especially if you were raised to ignore it. Especially if it kept the score for things no one else ever saw.

Maybe you were taught that your body was a problem to manage. That pain was an inconvenience. That endurance was character. Maybe rest only came after collapse—and even then, it felt like cheating.

But alignment doesn't require you to befriend your body overnight. It just invites you to stop fighting it.

You don't have to decode every ache or explain every symptom. But you do have to stop assuming your body is lying. That's the legacy so many of us inherited—especially if we grew up praised for pushing through. We learned that discomfort meant weakness. That expressing pain meant dramatics. That calm and composure were the only acceptable responses.

But your body isn't trying to trick you. It's trying to tell you the truth.

Start there.

Try noticing when your jaw tightens, when your shoulders hunch, when your stomach flips or your breath catches in your throat. Try asking, gently: "What is this sensation trying to tell me?"

Not with judgment. Not with urgency. Just with curiosity.

If the answer doesn't come right away, that's okay. You're building trust with a part of yourself that has been trying to get your attention for a long time.

For some people, listening to their body is a relief. For others, it's complicated. Especially if your body has been a battleground. If it's been dismissed. Exoticized. Regulated. If the world has made you feel like embodiment is a luxury you have to earn. This isn't about forcing a connection—it's about offering one. Slowly. Kindly.

One tool I often recommend is a simple body scan. Not to fix anything. Not to optimize. Just to notice.

When you learn to notice, something shifts. You stop overriding. You stop apologizing. You stop numbing. You begin to trust that the signals you've been calling inconvenient are actually invitations.

I used to see a massage therapist who only said three things during every session:

"Anything we should focus on today?"

"Is that too much pressure?"

"Okay, Kirk—we're done."

That was it. No small talk. No unsolicited advice. Just presence. Attunement. Respect.

He'd find knots I didn't know I had. Places I'd been clenching without realizing. And he didn't try to force anything—just worked with what was there, adjusting as needed.

It was the opposite of that other massage—the one with the therapist who told me about his daughter's softball team and his medication regimen while I lay half-naked, trying to disappear. That wasn't care. It was intrusion.

This? This was different.

Sometimes I think that's the kind of relationship I'm still trying to build with my body. One where I check in. Adjust. Don't bulldoze. Just listen.

And maybe whisper, "Okay—we're done," when it's time to rest.

START WITH NOTICING

If you've never listened to your body on purpose, it can feel awkward. Even silly. You might wonder, *Am I doing this right?* The answer is yes— if you're paying attention, you're doing it right.

You don't need candles or chants or a special mat. You just need a moment. A pause. Enough stillness to ask yourself: *What's happening in me right now?*

One of the gentlest ways to begin is with a body scan. Not a performance. Not a test. Just a check-in. A way of learning your own cues, in your own time.

Here's one way to try it:

- Find somewhere quiet—ish. It doesn't have to be silent. Life makes noise.
- Sit in a chair. Lie down. Take a walk. Whatever makes you feel a little more in your body than outside of it.
- Let your attention move slowly—from the top of your head to the tips of your toes.

Ask simple questions:

- *Where am I holding tension?*
- *What feels open? What feels braced?*
- *Am I breathing or just thinking about breathing?*

That's it. You don't need a breakthrough. You don't need a journal full of insights. Just start by noticing.

And if that feels like too much? Pick one part. Your hands. Your jaw. Your back. Ask: *What's here? What's needed?*

You don't have to do anything with the answer. But the asking itself is an act of respect.

For some people, this kind of noticing leads to peace. For others, it brings up fear. Especially if your body hasn't always felt like a safe place to live. Maybe you've carried trauma. Maybe your body has been judged or controlled or misunderstood. Maybe you were told to perform health instead of inhabit it.

If that's you, go slow. You're not behind. You're rebuilding trust.

You're remembering that your body is yours. That you get to listen without rushing in to fix. That presence isn't always calm—it's just *real*.

Some people feel tired after a body scan. Some cry. Some feel absolutely nothing. It's all valid. You're learning your own signals. That's the work.

Soul Audit: Embodiment & Listening

Before your mind can explain it, your body already knows. It tightens. Flinches. Shuts down. Or opens up. Alignment starts with paying attention to those signals—and refusing to dismiss them as overreactions.

Check all that apply:

- ☐ I override exhaustion with caffeine, pressure, or guilt
- ☐ I've ignored pain or tension because it was inconvenient
- ☐ I feel disconnected from my body unless something is wrong
- **☐ I can recognize physical signs that I'm misaligned**

- ☐ **I have practices that help me feel safe in my own skin**
- ☐ **I trust my body's discomfort as a signal—not a failure**

If any of these feel familiar, take a moment.

You're not doing it wrong. You're learning a new language. The more you notice, the more clearly your body speaks. You don't have to fix it. Just listen. It's been telling the truth this whole time.

FROM THE AUDIT TO ACTION

AWARENESS

You're not just a mind with a body attached. You are a whole system.

Alignment doesn't happen in your thoughts alone—it happens in your breath, your posture, your heartbeat, your ability to exhale.

Ask yourself:

- *When do I feel most present in my body—and when do I disappear?*
- *Where does my body tighten when I'm performing or pleasing?*
- *What physical sensation do I ignore most often—and what might it be pointing to?*
- *What would happen if I treated that discomfort as a message, not a malfunction?*

PRACTICE

This week, try a five-minute body scan. Sit still. Close your eyes. Breathe. Move slowly from head to toe and simply notice:

Where is there tension? Where is there ease?

Then ask: *What does this part of me need right now?*

You don't have to act on the answer. You just have to hear it.

The body doesn't lie. And it's not trying to hurt you. It's trying to help you find your way back home.

CHAPTER 17
WEIRDOS WELCOME

When I opened my first private practice—after leaving the job that paid me extra pennies instead of a merit raise—I didn't have a business loan, a startup grant, or an investor. I had a lease in a no-frills office building, a list of things I couldn't afford yet, and a handful of people who loved me enough to show up and help.

Cheryl and I had both left our jobs around the same time. She found a new position working in a hospital. I decided to hang up my own shingle. And while running a solo practice is relatively affordable once it's up and running, getting it off the ground required some capital—and a lot of stuff I didn't have. Furniture for both the lobby and the counseling room. A copier that could scan, fax, and probably make pancakes if I'd read the manual. Internet. Electricity. Paint.

I'm terrible at manual labor. *Work smarter, not harder* continued to be my mantra. So when I needed to paint the office and didn't know where to begin, I asked for help. And people showed up.

Cheryl came. So did our friend Cindy and her husband. "We love to paint," Cindy said. I don't know if that was true, but I was grateful regardless.

We had a painting party. I rolled and brushed and generally did a terrible job. At one point, I must have looked so pitiful that Cindy kindly said,

"Why don't you sit down and let us take care of this?" Weaponized incompetence on my part? Maybe. But real friendship on theirs.

Cheryl also loaned me the money I needed for liability insurance so I could see clients. She's shown up to every single play I've written. She's read all my books. She answers the phone when I need to talk after a long day. She lets me process out loud while I drive home. She holds space when I don't make sense yet.

We've gotten to the point where we text every morning, just to make sure we both woke up. I even set up a shortcut on my iPhone so that at 9:30 every morning, it automatically sends her a "good morning" text. She writes back. I reply with something funny or tired or unnecessary. And we both breathe a little easier.

I live alone. She lives alone. It's nice to know someone would notice if I didn't wake up. Before the smell alarmed the neighbors.

That's friendship. Not the curated Instagram version. The real kind. The kind where someone shows up with a paintbrush and a checkbook and says, "I've got you." The kind where you're allowed to be tired and scattered and weird and wrong sometimes. The kind that lets you be fully human and doesn't ask you to explain.

We don't talk enough about that kind of friendship. The spiritual kind. The chosen family kind. The kind that saves you—not all at once, but in a thousand small ways.

So this chapter is for the friends who show up and stay. For the ones who text good morning to make sure we're still here. For the people who hold the mirror when we forget who we are. This chapter is a thank you. And a welcome mat.

A WEIRD LITTLE LIFE

I've never been in a romantic relationship. I've never been on a date. That's something I talked about in *Jesus & Me*, and it's still true. What's also true is that it hasn't made my life less full—it's just made it different. Not lonelier. Not lesser. Just different.

There are times I wonder if something is wrong with me. If I missed a window. If I'm too weird, too complicated, too visible, too invisible. There's a lot of cultural noise that suggests romantic love is the prize at the end of the game—and if you don't win it, you're either broken or hiding.

But that's not how it's played out for me.

My life is full of people who show up. Not because they have to. But because they want to. People who know my weirdest habits, my worst moods, my laziest days—and love me anyway. People like Cheryl. Or Anne. Or Sharon. Tyler. Chad. DJ. Vince and Amy. The list is long.

And there's something profound about that.

To be honest, I'm not sure a romantic partner could offer me anything I don't already have in the people I call family. Would it be nice to split rent? Sure. Would it be nice not to always take out the trash? Absolutely. Would it be nice to have a regular intimate encounter with someone I know... well, intimately?

Of course. I'm 49—I'm not dead.

But emotionally? Spiritually? I'm not starving. I'm held.

I've built a life that looks a little strange from the outside. A weird little life, stitched together by theater kids and fellow therapists, former co-workers and new collaborators. People I text at midnight. People who show up at my play readings with snacks and applause. It's not curated. It's not clean. But it is deeply, wildly aligned.

I know who I am in the context of friendship. I know how I show up. I know what kind of support I offer, and what kind I need. And I've been lucky—maybe even blessed—to find people who meet me there. Without pretense. Without performance.

Romantic love might still happen someday. But if it doesn't? I'm good. Really good.

Because the people who love me now don't need a big declaration. Or a ring. Or a future timeline. They just need me to text them back. Maybe make them laugh. Maybe remind them to take their meds.

They're my people. I'm theirs. That's alignment. That's enough. That's the weird little life I get to live. And I wouldn't trade it for anything.

I think that's part of why shows like *Golden Girls, Designing Women, Friends, Will & Grace,* and even *The Office* meant so much to me growing up. They weren't just sitcoms—they were blueprints. Proof that **your people** didn't have to come from your bloodline or be tied to romance. They could be the ones who made you laugh, who showed up with takeout and sarcasm, who stuck around through awkwardness and grief and weird Thanksgiving traditions.

Chosen family isn't just possible. It's real. We just have to find them.

A YES TO THE TEA PARTY

Sophia had been a nurse for almost thirty years. She'd worked in the same small practice her entire career—same doctor, same office, same routine. She knew the patients by name. Knew their spouses, their kids, their prescriptions. She should've left years ago, but she didn't like change.

Sophia was shy. Painfully so. She always assumed people were talking about her, and not in a flattering way. I wouldn't go so far as to call her paranoid, but she definitely had her antenna up. And she was beyond lonely.

She'd been married once. Her husband cheated on her repeatedly until she finally left him—and she took half of everything. He never forgave her for that. And he didn't keep his resentment to himself. He tried to poison their four children against her. At least one of them believed that narrative. The others didn't call or visit very often, either.

Sophia didn't have a social life. She didn't go out. Her routine was work, home, TV, bed. She watched *Grey's Anatomy*, picked apart the medical details, and secretly wished she had co-workers like that. She didn't want the drama—but she envied the closeness. The shared lunches. The hugs in the hallway. Even the playful teasing.

When she first came to therapy, she could barely make eye contact with me. She spoke quietly, cautiously, and usually only to say something self-deprecating. But under all that silence, the flicker was still there. Her soul hadn't gone out—it had just dimmed.

I did what I do. I fanned the flame.

I affirmed her. Not with fake compliments, but with truth. Specific targeted strength-building. We talked about her work ethic, her incredible loyalty. I asked her what she might like to do, if she weren't so afraid of being disappointed. She said she'd like to have a friend. Just one. But she didn't know how to make that happen.

We talked about how friendship isn't something that arrives—it's something we make space for. And sometimes, it starts by being just a little more friendly.

After some gentle nudging, she decided to try going to church again. There was one nearby she'd driven past a thousand times. I held my breath—because, as you probably know, sometimes that goes really well. And sometimes it doesn't.

But this time, it worked.

On her second visit, the pastor's wife noticed her. Like approaching a wounded animal in the forest, she moved slowly. She smiled. Made small talk. Invited Sophia to the ladies' tea. And then to lunch. And then introduced her to a few other single women at the church—most of them older, most of them with similar stories.

And wouldn't you know it, Sophia made a friend. A couple, actually.

Watching her transform from someone who couldn't hold eye contact to someone making lunch plans was one of the most rewarding moments of my career.

Making friends didn't overhaul Sophia's life. But it shifted the temperature. It brought in a little warmth, a little light, and just enough connection to remind her that she wasn't too broken, or too awkward, or too late to the party.

She didn't reinvent herself. She didn't become the life of the party. She just got a little clearer about what she needed—and a little braver about showing up. That clarity—that willingness to be seen—was the beginning of alignment. Her outer life finally started to reflect her inner longing. That's what alignment looks like. It doesn't always roar. Sometimes, it starts by saying "yes" to a tea party.

QUICK CHECK-IN

Pause here. Take a breath.

- *Where have you felt too weird, too different, or too much to belong?*
- *Who are the people—past or present—who saw you and stayed?*
- *What parts of yourself have you been hiding in order to feel "normal"?*
- *What would it look like to stop waiting for approval and start building connection?*

You don't have to fit into some socially acceptable box to find your people. You just have to let yourself be known. Alignment isn't about blending in. It's about showing up fully—and letting yourself be loved anyway.

WHEN IT'S TIME TO LET GO

Not every friendship survives alignment—and not every person who calls themselves a friend is safe.

I've had to let go of a few friendships in my life—relationships that, on the surface, looked fine but were quietly siphoning my energy, my peace, and sometimes my money. Often, the imbalance was clear: I was giving too much. They were taking even more.

One friendship ended when the lies got so tangled, even they couldn't keep their stories straight. At one point, they created an entirely fake brother—complete with a social media account—and messaged me from it to manipulate the narrative. I'm still not sure why.

Another friend was using drugs. For over a year, he borrowed money from me—framing it as rent help, groceries, emergencies. In truth, he was funding his addiction. I didn't know until he broke into my apartment and stole my camera equipment. Then he texted me to confess what he'd done. Said he was going to rehab. I met with him one last time to close the loop. That was it. I was done.

These weren't just bad friends. They were unsafe people.

And naming that doesn't erase the good memories. It just tells the truth. Alignment asks you to stop twisting yourself into a version of friendship that serves other people's chaos. It asks you to get clear on what you need—and what you're no longer available for.

But how do you even tell when a friendship isn't aligned anymore?

Sometimes it's obvious—like the friend who lies, manipulates, or steals from you. But other times, it's quieter. A gut feeling you ignore. A pattern you explain away. A dynamic that once felt mutual but now leaves you tired, small, or vaguely ashamed.

Here's what I've learned to look for:

- You leave interactions feeling worse, not better
- You over-function in the relationship—always giving, rarely receiving
- You feel like you're performing rather than showing up as yourself
- You second-guess your words, your tone, your needs
- You realize you've stopped reaching out—but still feel guilty when they don't
- You feel alone in the friendship, even when you're technically not

This isn't failure. It's information.

Friendship should be honest. It should breathe. It should hold space for growth and change—not punish you for it. Aligned friendships may not be perfect, but they're real. They don't require constant management. They don't demand you shrink.

Sometimes the bravest thing you can do is tell the truth about a friendship that no longer fits—and let it go with clarity, not bitterness.

Because space cleared is space that can be filled.

And the weirdos you're waiting for? The ones who show up with paintbrushes and punchlines, snacks and soul-level presence? They need room to find you.

Let them in.

SOUL AUDIT: FRIENDSHIP & BELONGING

Friendship isn't extra credit. It's essential.

Aligned friendships let you exhale, be weird, and stay whole.

Misaligned ones shrink you. Twist you. Blur your reflection.

This audit helps you notice the difference.

Check all that apply:

- ☐ I feel like I have to edit myself in most of my friendships
- ☐ I've lost friendships that mattered deeply—and still carry grief or guilt
- ☐ I long for deeper connection but feel unsure how to get there
- **☐ I have at least one person who sees and accepts my full weirdness**
- **☐ I can name where I'm overfunctioning—and where I'm truly receiving**
- **☐ I believe chosen family is just as sacred as biological**

If any of these landed with you, take a moment. Notice what you're longing for. Notice where you feel most at home. Friendship doesn't require you to be perfect. Just present.

And the people who really get you? They'll be glad you showed up.

FROM THE AUDIT TO ACTION

Awareness

Friendship doesn't require you to be impressive. It asks you to be present. The right people will meet you where you are—not where you're pretending to be.

Ask yourself:

- *Where do I feel most at ease—and where do I feel on guard?*
- *Who has shown up for me without being asked?*
- *Where am I giving more than I'm receiving—and what is that costing me?*
- *What's one truth I've been afraid to say out loud in a friendship?*

PRACTICE

This week, try one of these:

- Text someone who makes you feel like yourself and say, "I really appreciate you."
- Notice where you're over-functioning—and gently step back.
- Make space for new connection by showing up just 10% more vulnerably in one conversation.
- Revisit a one-sided friendship and ask yourself: What do I need here—and am I willing to name it?

Weirdness isn't something to hide. It's a signal to your people. Let it shine.

CHAPTER 18
WHAT IF IT'S ALLOWED TO FEEL GOOD?

I STILL PLAY with my action figures.

I don't talk about it much, because I know it's weird. I grew up hearing that Bible verse—*"When I was a child, I spake as a child..."*—followed by the not-so-gentle reminder that it was time to "put away childish things." Shame baked right into the language. No room for joy unless it looked appropriately adult.

But on a lazy Sunday afternoon, I might pull out a handful of WWE figures and start planning an epic wrestling card. Everyone in the toybox has their own identity. Some of them are old G.I. Joe characters who've been repurposed into new roles. Some have entire histories I created from scratch. I could tell you their finishing moves, their greatest feuds, who their mentors were, and what storylines defined their careers.

It sounds ridiculous. And it probably is. But you know what? It brings me joy.

It brings me the kind of joy that doesn't need to be shared or posted or praised. The kind that's just mine. It's silly, imaginative, totally unnecessary—and completely aligned with who I am.

There's a particular kind of joy that comes from loving things without worrying what people think. Joy, for me, comes in the form of action figures. But also the PeopleMover at Magic Kingdom. It's hugging a friend outside a Broadway stage door. It's Kings Island—especially at Christmas. It's a perfect steak at the casino, delivered by a server who knows my name. It's RSVLTS shirts. It's photography. It's a text from a friend that just says "hey." It's writing a play that feels true—and hearing it performed out loud for the first time.

And the list goes on.

Joy is rarely flashy. It's often small. But it's never meaningless.

JOY IS THE EVIDENCE

I didn't always know joy was part of alignment. I used to think of it as a bonus—something extra that might show up after you'd done all the hard work. Once you set boundaries, grieved your losses, and got your life in order, maybe then, if you were lucky, joy would sneak in around the edges. But that's not what I've learned—not for myself, and certainly not in my work with clients.

Joy isn't a reward. It's a sign. It's what surfaces when you're living closer to your truth. When your nervous system starts to unclench. When you stop bracing for impact every time something good happens. It's not always loud, and it's not always tied to happiness in the traditional sense. But it is alive. You feel it in the unplanned laugh. In the moment you catch yourself humming without realizing it. In the quiet spark of actually looking forward to something. That's joy—and joy is information.

It can also be work, especially for people who've lived in survival mode for years. For those who were taught that joy is irresponsible, unearned, immature, or even sinful, it can feel dangerous. You'd be surprised how many people I've sat across from in therapy who freeze when I ask them one simple question: "What do you enjoy?"

They can name their fears. They can list what they're working on and what they're healing from. But ask what makes them light up, and they look away. Some say, "I don't know." Some say, "I used to love reading, but..." or "I guess I like music, but I don't have time anymore." And sometimes, they cry.

The absence of joy isn't just emotional flatness—it's a form of grief, especially when it's been disguised as *practicality*.

I had a client once who described her life as "functional but gray." She was a good parent, a hard worker, and a dependable employee. Her house was clean. Her calendar was full. But her spirit was flat. She hadn't felt joy in years, and every time we got close to the topic, she'd pivot back to logistics—her kid's IEP, her husband's anxiety, the latest meal prep plan.

One day, I asked her when she last felt silly. She paused, confused. "Silly?" she asked, like it was a foreign concept. "Yeah," I said. "Light. Unproductive. A little ridiculous. When's the last time you laughed so hard your stomach hurt?" She thought about it for a while and finally said, "High school, I think."

We didn't start with gratitude journaling or vision boards. We started with music. I asked what songs she loved at sixteen. She made a playlist. She played it in the car. A week later, she came in smiling and said, "I forgot how much I loved the Spice Girls." Then we spent the next five minutes laughing at how dumb some of those lyrics were. And that's where the joy started—not with a grand breakthrough, but with one ridiculous pop song that served as a reminder that her soul was still *in there*.

This is the kind of joy I'm talking about. Not performative happiness. Not toxic positivity. But the kind that quietly reminds you that you're still a person.

I've written before that you don't get to feel emotions selectively. If you numb sadness, you eventually numb joy, too. That's something I've lived. It's why I sometimes seek out sad plays or heavy movies—not to wallow, but to stretch. To soften. Sorrow creates space. And that space becomes the landing pad for joy.

Years ago, I used to DVR episodes of *Extreme Makeover: Home Edition* and save them for Sunday afternoons. I'd hold so much emotional weight during the week—clients' trauma, long days, the quiet loneliness of being the person others lean on—that by the time the weekend came around, I needed to feel something else. Those shows are designed to manipulate your emotions, of course, but I didn't care. Sad at the start, happy by the end—and I cried through every one of them. It gave me relief. A reset.

These days it's *Queer Eye*. I know the formula, I know where the edits are, but it doesn't matter. I cry anyway. Because it reminds me that people can change. That kindness matters. That joy isn't a luxury. It's necessary.

Alignment feels like a quiet shift toward the things that make me more human. Not just productive or responsible or stable—but alive. And when I notice joy, even in a fleeting way, I take it seriously. I see it as proof that I'm not just surviving. I'm connected. To myself. To the people who matter. To the life I've built.

PRACTICING JOY (ON PURPOSE)

If joy feels far away, start small. Don't wait for a grand passion to reappear. Don't put pressure on yourself to "find your bliss" or suddenly light up at everything. Just look for the flickers. Then fan the flame.

One way I help clients reconnect with joy is through a list I call *micro-joys*. These aren't hobbies or big plans. They're small, ordinary things that spark something—a smile, a breath, a softening. The key is that they feel good *to you*. Not to your social media feed. Not to your inner critic. Not to the version of yourself that thinks everything needs to be productive. Just you.

Here's how to build your own:

Set a timer for five minutes. Then make a list of *anything* that brings you a tiny bit of joy. Silly things. Sensory things. Nostalgic things. Even things you haven't done in years. Nothing is too small or too weird.

- Do you like the smell of new books?
- Watching baking videos even though you never bake?
- The way certain socks feel?

Great. Write it down. Your list might include:

- Listening to 90s country radio on a drive
- Organizing a junk drawer while watching old sitcoms
- Coloring with markers
- Eating buttered popcorn alone in the dark
- Visiting a candle store just to smell stuff
- Watching videos of flash mobs or surprise reunions
- Rearranging a room, just a little
- Going to Target with no agenda
- Sending a dumb meme to someone who gets it

The point isn't the content. It's the *connection*—to something inside you that says, *"I like this."*

After you've made your list, pick one thing. Try it. Not as a to-do. Not as a reward. Just as a practice. Just to see what happens when you allow joy a seat at the table again.

And if it doesn't work the first time? That's okay. Joy can be shy. Sometimes it takes a few invitations before it shows up.

But when it does? That's alignment. And it's worth practicing, especially if you grew up in a home where joy was seen as indulgent or even dangerous. You may have internalized the idea that delight is suspect.

But you're allowed to feel good—even without a reason.

SOUL AUDIT: JOY

Joy isn't a reward for getting everything right. It's a reminder that you're still alive. Still open. Still human. And alignment makes space for that.

Check all that apply:

- ☐ I feel guilty when I enjoy something "unproductive"
- ☐ I struggle to relax without justifying it first
- ☐ I've experienced joy recently—but felt the need to explain it or tone it down
- **☐ I can name something small that delights me, just because it does**
- **☐ I'm learning that joy is part of healing—not a detour from it**
- **☐ I believe pleasure, play, and presence belong in my life**

If any of these resonate, pause for a moment.

What does it stir in you to admit that joy might not need to be earned? That it might be part of your healing—not a distraction from it?

Joy doesn't need a reason. But it does need a welcome

FROM THE AUDIT TO ACTION

Awareness

Joy is more than an emotion—it's an instinct.

(And sometimes, it's a rebellion.)

Ask yourself:

- *What's one small thing that sparks a smile, a laugh, or a flicker of lightness?*

- *Where have you found yourself shrinking joy to seem more "serious" or "mature"?*
- *When was the last time you let yourself enjoy something freely, without apology?*

Joy doesn't need a permission slip. But if you're looking for one, here it is.

PRACTICE

Pick one small thing this week that delights you—and let yourself *amplify* it.

Examples:

- *If cheesy pop songs lift your mood, sing at the top of your lungs.*
- *If a certain coffee shop feels like a sanctuary, linger there.*
- *If you love goofy socks, wear them boldly and on purpose.*

Joy isn't the opposite of healing. It's the evidence that healing is happening.

Practice being someone who lets joy have a permanent place here. Even if it looks a little ridiculous. Even if it involves action figures. Especially then.

CHAPTER 19
STILL BECOMING

INTEGRATION IS one of those corporate buzzwords that feels kind of boring. It's also the crux of soul alignment.

But often when it happens, there's often no grand reveal. No triumphant soundtrack. No spiritual fireworks exploding over a mountaintop. Just you living your life with a little more honesty. A little more softness. A little more ability to notice when you're off—and maybe course-correct before everything implodes.

That's it. That's integration.

It's not an achievement. It's not a final exam. It's not a therapist handing you a certificate and saying, "Congratulations, you're now fully aligned." (If it was, I'd print them on thick cardstock and give them out with a commemorative pin. Maybe a tote bag.)

But that's not how this works. Integration isn't something you master. It's something you practice.

And that can be deeply annoying—especially if you, like me, love a checklist. Something to measure. Something to get an A in. But this process isn't about perfection—it's about progress.

And progress is measured in intensity, frequency, and duration. Ask yourself: When the misaligned moments show up (and they will), are

213

they happening less often? Are they less intense? Do they pass more quickly than they used to?

It's not always profound. Sometimes it just feels like *less hiding*. Like not spinning out for three days over something that used to take you out for a week. Like catching the old pattern before it drives the bus. Like making a sandwich instead of making a scene.

And listen, I know that's not going to trend on social media. No one wants to read a memoir called *Less Hiding and Fewer Emotional Spirals: My Journey to Being Basically Okay*. But that's what this chapter is. It's not a recap. It's not a resolution. It's an honest look at what it means to keep showing up when the dust settles.

Because after all this reflection, and grief, and unlearning, the question becomes: now what?

THE BORING MAGIC

There are five things I ask almost every client to prioritize. They're not revolutionary. They won't go viral as a morning routine. No one's putting them on a T-shirt with a catchy font. But they're the most reliable foundation I know. And they're always the first to go when life gets hard.

Here they are:

1. **Sleep.** Not just collapsing at 2 a.m. with the TV still on. Actual rest. The kind that lets your brain do maintenance work instead of replaying all your worst moments from eighth grade. The kind that whispers safety to your nervous system instead of panic.
2. **Body fuel.** Eat food. Real food. Not vibes and caffeine. Not guilt-laced protein bars that taste like drywall. Just

nourishment. Something that helps you function and feel like a person. And maybe drink some water once in a while.

3. **Body movement.** Not CrossFit. Not revenge abs. Just move. Walk. Stretch. Dance terribly in your kitchen. Stand up when your smartwatch tells you to. Feel your body carry you— because it still does, even when you ignore it.

4. **Sunlight.** I don't care if it's for five minutes. Go outside. Touch some grass. Look at a tree. Your circadian rhythm needs it, and so does your mood. Even a window counts. Let your skin remember the world exists.

5. **Interpersonal connection.** Talk to someone. Not in a crisis, but regularly. Someone who knows your middle name, or at least how your week's been. You don't need fifty friends. You need one person who wouldn't be totally chill if you disappeared.

Nine times out of ten, when someone tells me they're spiraling or feeling "off," at least one of these has fallen through the cracks.

This is the boring magic. It's not glamorous, but it works. And when these five things are in place, everything else becomes just a little easier to reach.

It's not a fix. It's a foundation.

WHEN YOU DON'T HAVE TIME FOR A SOUL AUDIT

Those five things—sleep, fuel, movement, sunlight, and connection— are my go-to checklist when things start to feel off. They're the foundation. But sometimes, I need something faster. Something I can run through in ten seconds when I feel myself spiraling or shutting down.

That's when I use **HALT**.

It's the simplest question I know:

- **Am I Hungry?**
- **Am I Anxious?**
- **Am I Lonely?**
- **Am I Tired?**

That's it. Four questions. No journal required. No breakthrough necessary.

Because the problem isn't always a deep emotional wound or a buried childhood trauma. Sometimes, I just need a sandwich. Or a nap. Or to hear someone say, "Yeah, that sucks."

HALT reminds me I don't have to solve everything. I just have to notice what's happening. It slows me down enough to remember I have options. I can breathe. I can pause. I can choose what comes next—without spiraling, without shame.

THE HEEL AND THE HEALER

Sometimes, soul alignment isn't about managing your physical needs. It's about making peace with your contradictions—the parts of you that don't make sense next to each other. The parts you thought you had to choose between.

Because authentic integration doesn't mean becoming one polished, unified version of yourself. It means holding all the versions that got you here—and learning how to let them coexist without blowing up your life.

That's where things get weird. For instance, the juxtaposition of being both a therapist and a professional wrestling heel was never lost on me.

In the ring, I cheated. I lied. I ranted. I abused. My character was unapologetically misaligned—and he was good at it. People believed me and people hated me, which was my goal. He was the kind of guy you desperately wanted to see get punched in the face.

And then on Monday morning, I'd walk into my counseling office where people cried in front of me and asked for help. Where I offered warmth and a listening ear instead of the bluster of my wrestling character.

Behind the scenes in the Northern Wrestling Federation, they called me "Bitterman." Not just because of the character, but because I was... well, bitter. Angry. I demanded perfection from people who were still learning. I had little patience for mistakes. If you were in the ring, I expected you to deliver. And when you didn't, I let you know—loudly and publicly.

I know people didn't like me. Some were afraid of me.

And yet—clients have told me, "I never thought I'd work with a male therapist, but I felt safe with you the minute you greeted me in the lobby." I've received cards that say, "You helped me feel seen in a way no one else ever has."

So how did these two versions of me coexist?

And more importantly—how did they eventually integrate?

The truth is, I still have strong opinions about wrestling. I still care about performance. I still feel that flicker of fury when someone phones it in. But when I visit now, I'm not Bitterman anymore. I'm not on the card. What happens in the ring is no longer a reflection of my backstage work. So, instead I offer guidance. I share wisdom. I root for people to do well.

And when a client shares something devastating—when they talk about being abused, exploited, abandoned—I sometimes say, "I'm going to maintain professionalism here... but know that a part of me wants to drag that person around the parking lot tied to the bumper of my car."

They usually laugh. But they also breathe a little easier.

Is that integration?

Maybe. Or maybe it's just honesty. Maybe it's recognizing that healing doesn't mean amputating your past. It means understanding what each version of you was protecting—and finding a way to let them all sit at the same table now.

That's what integration really is: letting the therapist and the heel coexist. No one has to get kicked out.

SOUL AUDIT: INTEGRATION

You don't have to be fully healed to be fully real.

Integration isn't about perfection—it's about learning how to return to yourself, again and again.

Check all that apply:

- ☐ I feel like different versions of me automatically show up in different roles
- ☐ I still try to "get it right" instead of being real
- ☐ **I've made peace with at least one version of myself I used to avoid**
- ☐ **I return to the same grounding practices when I feel off**
- ☐ **I can feel the difference between performing and belonging**
- ☐ **I believe progress is about noticing faster—not getting it perfect**

If any of these landed with you, take a breath. You're not failing—you're unfolding. Integration isn't about arriving. It's about noticing when you've drifted and gently coming back.

You don't need to evict anyone. Just make space at the table.

FROM THE AUDIT TO ACTION

AWARENESS

Integration doesn't look like a glow-up. It looks like a person who knows how to get back to themselves. The point isn't to stay perfectly aligned at all times. The point is to notice faster, and return with less shame.

Ask yourself:

- *When I feel off, do I notice—or just push through?*
- *What part of myself have I been trying to outrun?*
- *Where do I still think I have to earn my worth?*
- *What signals tell me I'm coming back into alignment?*

PRACTICE

This week, try treating misalignment as information—not failure.

- *Use HALT when you're irritable or spinning out*
- *Revisit your foundation: rest, nourishment, movement, sunlight, and connection.*
- *Say out loud, "This isn't the most aligned version of me, but I know how to get back"*
- *Let one part of you be messy, and don't apologize for it.*

Integration isn't about becoming someone else. It's about becoming *all of you,* and learning to stay.

You've survived. You've shifted. You're still becoming—and that's more than enough.

CHAPTER 20
THIS IS IT (PROBABLY)

I TOYED with calling this chapter *A Whole-Ass Life*. But I still worry that bad language might get me in trouble.

And honestly, that's kind of the point.

I'm still aligning. Still becoming. Still figuring out which parts of me get to take up space—and which ones are just trying to keep me safe. Still deciding when to say the thing and when to hold it. Still catching myself mid-pattern. Still feeling shame, even when I *know* it's okay to say "ass."

That's not failure. That's life. My life. Messy. Mostly-aligned. Wonderfully in progress.

There's no final form. No magical moment where everything clicks and stays clicked forever. No neon sign that says, *CONGRATULATIONS, YOU ARE NOW FULLY AUTHENTIC.*

There's just you. Living. Checking in. Re-adjusting. Auditing as needed.

Some days it feels easy. Other days it's forehead-against-the-steering-wheel hard. But alignment was never about getting it perfect. It's about coming back—with honesty, with compassion, with a little less hiding than the time before.

Aligning the soul isn't a destination. It's more like posture. It slips, you adjust, and eventually, it slips again. That doesn't mean you've failed. It just means you're still alive.

So I can't tell you what your aligned life should look like. I don't know what values you'll choose or what relationships you'll need to reevaluate. I don't know what truths you're only just beginning to tell.

But I do know this: if you've made it this far, you're already doing the work.

If you've been paying attention to what hurts, what delights you, where you've been pretending—that's motion. That's coming home to yourself, even if it's been a while.

For me, alignment rarely arrives as a lightning bolt. Instead, it's more like rolling thunder. It shows up in the quiet moments. When I enjoy something without needing to earn it first. When I pause before reacting. When I laugh during a moment that might've undone me a few years ago.

That's when I realize: something's different. I'm not performing. I'm just... here.

There's no trophy. No A+. No bonus points for figuring it out faster than someone else.

But there is joy in noticing the shift.

There's peace in realizing you no longer betray yourself as quickly.

That you bounce back a little sooner.

That you don't abandon your needs quite so easily.

And sometimes—on a good day—you look around at your weird, flawed, beautiful life and think:

Oh. This actually feels like mine.

DON'T GET SENTIMENTAL, DUMBASS

Ruthie didn't cry.

Ruthie—my client with the mangled hand, the sharp tongue, and the kind of heavy history that doesn't make for polite conversation—had been through things no one should have to endure. And she carried it all the way she carried everything else: tight, guarded, and with exactly zero tolerance for pity.

Trust didn't come easy to Ruthie. Vulnerability wasn't her language. In early sessions, she'd steal my chair just to see how I'd react. She called me names. Challenged every question like it came with strings attached. But she kept showing up. Week after week. Which, in her own twisted way, was its own kind of honesty.

She'd lost several fingers before I ever met her. We didn't dwell on the injury, but it was always there—part metaphor, part reminder. Ruthie didn't cry. She joked. She jabbed. She turned pain into punchlines, because that's how she stayed in control.

Then one day, the wall cracked.

We weren't even talking about anything new—just another loop through her week—when she went quiet. Her face shifted. Her jaw unclenched. And the tears came.

Not performative tears. Not controlled. These were the kind that rise up when your body finally stops fighting.

Mid-sentence, it hit her: the fingers weren't coming back. Not now. Not ever. And for just a moment, she let herself feel it. No speech. No breakdown. Just a slow, silent grief that took over her whole posture.

It was heartbreak. It was clarity. And it was trust—because she let it happen in front of me. Me, the dumbass who kept holding space for her. Me, the one who didn't flinch when she swore or snapped or tried to win therapy like it was a debate club.

That moment was the highest compliment Ruthie ever gave me.

And then—because of course she did—she wiped her face, snorted, and said, *"Don't get all sentimental about it, dumbass."*

That was Ruthie. She could grieve the loss of one hand and flip you off with the other.

But something shifted that day. Just slightly. Something in her stopped fighting long enough to be real.

And I think that's what integration looks like—not healing with a capital H, not a total transformation, but a flicker of truth. A breath of honesty. Just enough to remind you: *you're still here.*

And *you're still human.*

PROBABLY

I don't know how to end this book.

For a long time, I thought it needed something profound—some final moment of insight that would tie everything together in one beautiful metaphor.

We've covered a lot. We talked about identity and what it means to be fully yourself in a world that would rather you weren't. We looked at values—not the ones you inherited, but the ones you've chosen. We explored hard feelings like anger and shame, and how they're not problems to fix but signals to listen to. We walked through boundaries, time, spirituality, the body, grief, joy, and friendship—not because those are the only areas that matter, but because they're the places where misalignment tends to sneak in quietly and build a home.

And we talked about what happens when things begin to click—not perfectly, but just enough. Just enough to feel like you're good.

Not extraordinary. Not epiphanic. Just... good.

Today, I met with clients I genuinely enjoy. I hid in the group room for twenty minutes with my feet up on the sofa and my eyes closed. I went outside for five minutes and walked around the building even though I didn't want to. I drank water instead of Coke. I mean, I still had a Coke. But I drank water, too. I ignored an email I didn't want to respond to—and didn't feel guilty about it. I listened to a podcast on the way home. Got the mail. Dealt with a burnt-out lightbulb.

None of it was headline-worthy. None of it would make a compelling Instagram reel.

But it all felt like enough.

And maybe that's the whole point.

Maybe alignment isn't something we arrive at, but something we get better at noticing. Maybe a whole, human life doesn't need to be loud or big or certain—it just needs to be real. Present. Practiced. Reclaimed one honest choice at a time.

Maybe this is it. Probably?

And that's totally enough.

TURNS OUT IT WASN'T

During the final editing process, I found myself hesitant to re-read the book from cover to cover. I was afraid I'd discover just how poorly written it really was—or worse, realize I'm an actual fraud. But after journaling about it (and a few conversations with my AI writing partner), I remembered: this is exactly what I wrote about.

Vulnerability. Imperfection. The willingness to stay open even when it's uncomfortable.

Instead of reading my book as a critic, I decided to read it as a celebration.

And then I choked back tears in Gold Star Chili. I looked around at the formica tables and the fluorescent lights and thought: this is exactly what soul alignment feels like. Not perfect or polished. Just authentic.

It doesn't get realer than that.

I know, realer isn't a word. I'm leaving it anyway.

ACKNOWLEDGMENTS

It struck me, at some point, that I needed a book I could hand to a client —or anyone, really—that embodied the things I say almost every day. The truths I've collected over two decades of sitting with people. The patterns I've seen. The wisdom that shows up in ordinary moments.

This is that book.

After twenty-one years of practice, I've realized that while the details of our lives may differ, the themes are remarkably consistent: shame, grief, identity, longing, boundaries, forgiveness, joy. I also realized that I've been writing a mental-health–themed blog every week for years—and that content deserved a bigger stage. So I turned to ChatGPT for help organizing and categorizing it all, and together we crafted this collection of story, insight, humor, and hope.

Writing it has been cathartic. And healing. And, honestly, kind of fun. I'm proud of it. And if it helps even one person feel more seen, more understood, or more whole—then it's worth it.

Special thanks to my friends "Cheryl," Sharon, LaShanda, as well as "Ruthie," "Debby," and all the other clients—real, fictionalized, or somewhere in between—who have taught me about people. Thank you for letting me learn alongside you.

Thanks to Brené Brown for her revolutionary work in the areas of shame, vulnerability, and emotional truth. Her voice gave mine permission.

Thanks to the crew at Gold Star Chili—and to Betty Jo—for offering me a writing sanctuary, a steady stream of Coke, and just enough human interaction to keep me grounded. This book has grease stains and shredded cheese baked into its pages, and I wouldn't have it any other way.

To Vince and Amy—thank you for your steady, consistent encouragement. You believe in me, and your validation is beyond anything I could imagine.

To Jensen, Cassie & Sean, Piper, Sheri, Annika, Ry, and Ros—and everyone else who came to the release party for the previous two books —thank you for making that night unforgettable. And to Kayla, Emmy, Nancy, Marian, and all the others who've reached out about my work and its effect on their lives: thank you for seeing me. Your words have given me the confidence to keep writing.

To William Shakespeare: I don't like your shows, but I respect your work. You're the literary equivalent of spinach—important, good for me, but not nearly as fun as carbs. Or Andrew Lloyd Webber.

To Mickey Mouse: You've given me joy when I needed it most. That's enough.

And thank you—yes, *you*—for reading this. For being curious. For showing up to the work. For wanting to live in closer alignment with who you really are. That's brave. And beautiful. And it matters.

Buy a copy for someone you love. Or someone you hate. Whatever works. And if you find any typos, I probably put them there on purpose. (Or not, but you'll never know.)

Thanks for reading.

Now, go be weird. Go be wonderful. (Same thing, really.)

ABOUT THE AUTHOR

Kirk Sheppard is a licensed therapist, writer, playwright, and lifelong collector of good stories. With over two decades of experience in mental health, he brings warmth, clarity, and a touch of irreverence to conversations about shame, identity, grief, and what it means to live in alignment. He's the author of *Jesus & Me*, *The Search Party*, and *Soul Audit*, and has written a weekly blog on personal growth and mental health for years.

He lives in Cincinnati, Ohio, writing in Gold Star booths (burgers only, no chili), drinking regular Coke, and quoting *The Office* with alarming regularity in therapy sessions. His work invites readers to be honest, not perfect—and to build lives that feel like their own.

More at kirksheppard.com and the links below.

facebook.com/kirkthecounselor
instagram.com/kirk.sheppard.writer